To

With eternal (if you'll forgive me!) gratitude.

Beyond Our Means
Poetry, Prose and Blue Runes

For the wound and the gift summer gave

And I tell myself, a moon will rise from my darkness
– Mahmoud Darwish, Palestinian poet

The cover image is adapted and developed from a photograph by Lesley Wall, reproduced with deep gratitude. The spiral moon, which is itself a reflection to us of light from the sun, radiates through the portal of night and the canopy provided by the tree's branches. At once soft and strong, gentle and explosive, the colour used for this adaptation of the original image is drawn from a spectrum generated by the camera. Many layers of meaning and possibility lie within this process and the resulting impressions, both natural and mechanical. It is definitely the habitus of blue runes.

Bonfire Moon

Light streams through the green fuse
Each blond ray unwrapped from a
sun always lifting and warming.
Let this spiralled winter moon
embrace and magnify all of
your dreams, hopes and
wishes for this year…

Beyond Our Means
Poetry, Prose and Blue Runes

Simon Barrow

First published in January 2025

Siglum Publishing
Edinburgh
Scotland
www.siglumpublishing.co.uk

Copyright © Simon Barrow

The right of Simon Barrow to be identified as the author and creator of this work is asserted in accordance with Section 77 of the Copyright, Designs and Patents Act 1998.

Photographs and images are used with permission or license and are the copyright of their creators.

Production and design: Bob Carling
Editorial: Gillian Stern
Author photo: Hazel Dunlop
Front cover photo: Lesley Maria Wall
Back cover skyscape: Sonny Mauricio @northernstatemedia

ISBN: 978-1-9161733-3-0

A Catalogue record for this book is available from the British Library

Contents

Preface		xi
Introduction: On Being Broken by Words		xiii
PART ONE		1
Living Beyond Our Moments		1
I	Unprosaic	9
II	Found	13
III	Wordcraft	17
IV	Blue Mountains	21
V	(Un)quiet Heart	25
VI	Gonebye	29
VII	Art Forms	33
VIII	Beyond Likeness	37
IX	Wired (Blue Guitar)	41
X	Unnaming	45
XI	Spiral Reasons	49
XII	Lifesigns	51

PART TWO			55
Living Beyond Our Masks			55
	XIII	Before Words	63
	XIV	Embracing Light	67
	XV	We Have Now	71
	XVI	Your People Will Find You	75
	XVII	Blue Advent Rose	79
	XVIII	Acceptance	83
	XIX	Unspent	87
	XX	Shot Sage Blue Marilyn (Reframed)	91
	XXI	Mystique	95
	XXII	Orpheus Untold	99
	XXIII	Candy and Dust	103
	XXIV	Reconnected	107
PART THREE			111
Living Beyond Our Means			111
	XXV	Wakeful Poetry	121
	XXVI	Childless	125
	XXVII	Blue Runes	129
	XXVIII	Lightshadows	133
	XXIX	Deep Time	137
	XXX	Yearnings	143
	XXXI	Unwounding	147
	XXXII	Ante-supper	151
	XXXIII	Pierced Beauty	155

XXXIV	Autumnising	159
XXXV	Lakesong	161
XXXVI	Transfigured	167

Aftersong: Poems (Mostly) Without Words	171
Further Reading	181
Acknowledgements	189
About the Author	193
Winter Sun	195

Preface

THIS BOOK houses 44 new poems in total, plus 36 short prose pieces, four essays, and an introductory chapter – all previously unpublished. Aside from two seasonal verses that open and close the collection, these poems are divided into equal sections of 12. Each section (parts one, two and three) is prefaced by an essay, and each individual poem is followed by an accompanying piece of prose. Then there are the secrets and half-secrets. The runes within the ruminations. One poem is actually two. Three are embedded within the main section essays. Other unexpected appearances may discover the attentive, too.

The idea of accompanying poems with prose came after the verses themselves had been written. A few reveal or acknowledge sources and inspirations, or go into a little detail about form and structure. That only happens where I think it may help the reader (rather than the poem), particularly with aspects which initially appear obscure or obtuse.

Sometimes poetry presents itself as a 'take it or leave it' private craft. Inevitably, there are personal as well as public meanings within it, including public ones that may pass the reader by. But I am resistant to the idea that a poem is or should be a code to crack. Though if you want to read T. S. Eliot, it's true, you will find it difficult if not impossible without being able to recognise or discover a web of literary and historical references.

I am not remotely in Eliot's league (or that of my other poetic heroes, including the peerless Dylan Thomas), but some of the verses here do have layers of reference or allusion which work somewhat in that way. Others are more straightforward. Many float between different worlds. All are meant to be read aloud. I have my own voice, but my style, tone, word-use and textural choices vary. There are word-eliding neologisms, too.

I do not apologise for any of that. But I hope the prose accompaniments, without 'translating' the verse (why not just stick to prose, if you can do that?), provide some context for the poems they follow, offering clues and thoughts which will help them connect, whether aesthetically, semantically, transcendentally, or all three.

Introduction

On Being Broken by Words

All that was Beauty, all that was Love, all that was Truth, stood on top of these mad mornings and sang with the stars.
– W. E. B. Du Bois[1]

LIFE WILL BREAK YOU, Louise Erdrich[2] reminds us. Words will break you, too. Poetry, especially, nearly always involves a breaking process – because poetry is the most creatively and threateningly broken form language can take. But it is not about pain or heartbreak alone. It is also about the in-breaking of light, the possibility of breaking the chains that bind, and the breaking down of wilful or unknowing resistance to beauty, truth, goodness, faith, hope and love wherever they are to be found. That is often in places, people and possibilities 'beyond our means'. Thus my title.

Having spent years heavily invested in the interrogations and commitments of politics, philosophy, ethics, and what passes for 'religion' in Christian and other senses, I wanted in this collection to stand back and think about our lives – and life as a whole – as shared gift and possibility. I slightly hesitate to use the word 'spirituality' to describe this venture, because that can so easily degenerate into indulgent introspection. But re-engagement with

---

1 A much-quoted phrase that derives from W. E. B. Du Bois, *Black Reconstruction in America* (Free Press, 1999; first published in 1935). It is important to recognise that its referent is the experience of emancipation among slaves. In the midst of a historical argument about liberation, Du Bois could not but reach for poetic and biblical-style language which is in and of itself poetry. Good poetry must always set us free, if it connects.
2 See, among the other extraordinary works of this prize winning Native American writer, Louise Erdrich, *Original Fire: Selected and New Poems* (Harper, 2004).

all that lives, moves and has its being alongside us is certainly at the heart of these verses. In poetry and music we find fresh resources for flourishing in the face of pain or dislocation. My aim is to explore how this might be possible in different ways for each of us. For you as well as for me.

Much of what presses us towards the poetic is outwith our control in the way it impresses itself upon us or invites us into its presence and promise. These riddle-like occurrences are what I call 'blue runes', and they surface throughout this collection, especially in poems palpably connected to blueness – the colour of imagination, intuition, deep soulfulness, and the sheer expanse of sky and sea. Runes are phonetic symbols, similar to letters, derived from early Germanic languages and signifying many families of meaning ahead of the formal arrival of words. They are simultaneously symbols of connection and anticipation. The heart of poetry, I would suggest, is indeed "reading the runes". Not to conjure up magic spells, but as a path into the web of meaning within, beyond and before the interplay of linguistic surfaces.

The dedication at the beginning of this book is about a particular and personal breaking process. The wound and the gift summer gave, arising from a special moment of encounter, has broken me into daily pieces ever since. Deep in my heart, I knew it would. But I had neither the wit nor the courage to avoid it. That is why, in the poem that seeded the idea for this collection, I put gift and wound together. The gift came first. Casually, then startlingly, then alongside a lurking, growing fear. The fear was of loss. And it came. Effectively on the very day of summer solstice, exactly one year later. There will be someone reading this (or perhaps not) who will know the poem to which I refer. Will the wound give way to healing and repair? Time, the focus of the first essay in this book, always suspends itself in the waiting. Meanwhile, as I indicate later, we have now.

That personal fracture apart (one which seemed to block me from finishing the prose pieces contained herein for nearly four months), the creation of this small volume has also been accompanied by the unbearable stench of mass slaughter in Gaza, extend-

Introduction: On Being Broken by Words

ing to Lebanon: one of the great centres of poetry in the Middle East. This has been not so much a breaking process as a series of acts of wanton destruction and hate, well beyond revenge, rooted in decades of oppression and a spiral of violence. Poetry always has much to say in facing personal pain. But what of the world of politics, conflict, war, terror, collective punishment and genocide? Words fail at such junctures. But the ones which fail best are usually found in verse.[3]

There is one poem in this collection which addresses the trauma of Palestine-Israel directly. But despite my own engagements, and a sense of guilt about it, if I am honest, political poetry has almost completely eluded me in this book. For the time being, at least. Trump has left me numb. Others (such as Lebanese poet Nadia Tuéni)[4] have already said or are presently saying (as with Scottish academic and activist Alison Phipps)[5] what is needed. And they seem to say it so much better than I feel I ever could, because they fuse words out of the very tissue of the suffering they address. I prefer to dodge suffering, I fear.

In Christophe Ippolito's words, Nadia Tuéni "creates a sacred river that irrigates her poems", without suppressing either the rage or the frustration which may naturally accompany it. Likewise, Alison Phipps has responded with unfathomable anguish, with powerful gestures of protest, and with a deep longing for peace with justice. Her words cannot but be a form of prayer. Nothing less will suffice as the bombs and missiles continue to rain down. So my best contribution here is probably anguished, respectful poetic silence. That said, the three essays that preface the three sections of this book do move into political territory, the last so strongly. I have also drawn explicitly upon my own Christian formation in a number of places, though hopefully in a way that is open to those of other convictions and life stances.

---

3   F. R. Leavis is among those who rightly recognise that poetic language is inherently political and subversive because it undermines a technocratic, industrialised, financialised society.
4   Nadia Tuéni, *Lebanon: Poems of Love and War* (Syracuse University Press, May 2006).
5   Alison Phipps, *Call and No Response: 30 Prayers in Genocidal Times* (Wild Goose Publications, 2024). https://www.ionabooks.com/authors/phipps-alison/

Beyond Our Means

For my part, "standing atop these mad mornings" (Du Bois) has meant attending to the kind of beauty which alone can save the world (Fyodor Dostoevsky),[6] to truths that can break a heart of stone and turn it to flesh,[7] and to goodness in unexpected places that bypasses all our cunning plans and postures. I hope that, at least, becomes clear as you read on. Some of my more abstract verses are, I realise, probably overburdened with meanings (including the kind that elude me, also), while others are abjectly simple. I have tried only to write as the words, thoughts and feelings fall. Take what chimes, and leave the rest to sound elsewhere. That is the best advice I can give the reader.

The short essays on living beyond our moments, our masks and our means are somewhat related to the poems selected for the three sections of the book, but not in a programmatic way. There is much more (and better) that could be said on each. As for the prose that follows (or surrounds) each poem: its purpose is not to explain the verse *per se*, but to provide additional context, clues and conditions. Without, I hope, being too didactic, there are also some indications in those pieces about the choices and connections I made in composing each poem as I did. The overarching adopted 'style' – if it can be so called – is free verse. But that freedom arises from and requires certain disciplines acquired from a good deal of reading over the years, and from lessons taught by earlier failures with poetry.

You may well think that I have not yet learned enough from either the reading or the failures, but I hope there are some words in this book which connect with you, whoever you are. My wish is that everyone should meet and commune with their inner (and perhaps outer) poet, without fear or embarrassment. Because amidst the breaking up and the breaking down, of which there is a great

---

6 For further exposition, see my essay on 'Living Beyond Our Means' in this volume, along with the prose reflection accompanying 'Candy and Dust'. Also, David Fideler, 'How Beauty Can Save Us' in *Living Ideas Journal* (n.d.) https://livingideasjournal.com/how-beauty-can-save-the-world/ and David Bentley Hart, *The Beauty of the Infinite* (Eerdmans, 2003).
7 Gillian Court, *Heart of Flesh* (CTBI, 2008).

Introduction: On Being Broken by Words

deal in life, there is so much treasure to be found. In fragments, yes. But fragments that burst with moonlight and more.

> *Even so…*
> *I sing with the stars*
> *Through darkness*
> *the light refracted*
> *fractured, frozen*
> *moon scattered*
> *yet somehow*
> *undimmed*
> *How so… ?*[8]

In summary, next to (indeed, closely akin to) the more familiar explorative forms of philosophy and theology, it is poetry – along with many expanding waves of music explored in the afterword – that has become for me the most economical, expressive and demandingly unguarded way of navigating the ocean of feeling, reaching and unveiling within which we all "live and move and have our being". That phrase. It will recur, along with several others.

As Ursula Le Guin puts it: "Words are events, they do things, change things. They transform both speaker and hearer; they feed energy back and forth and amplify it. They feed understanding or emotion back and forth and amplify it."[9]

I can only trust that some of that energy is present for you in what follows.

Simon Barrow
The Feast of St Simon and St Jude
28 October 2024

---

8 My poem, entitled 'Even so… How so… ?'
9 Ursula K. Le Guin, *The Wave in the Mind: Talks and Essays on the Writer, the Reader, and the Imagination* (Shambhala Publications Inc., 2004).

PART ONE

Living Beyond Our Moments

*At the mid hour of night, when stars are weeping, I fly
To the lone vale we loved.* – Thomas Moore[1]

WORDS ARE WITH US, poetically and prosaically, but then they trail away. Like them, we need to be alive in the moment. Indeed, it is the only place we can possibly live. But we also need to have lived before and beyond the moment in order for the moment to have a meaning and a substantiating context, and it is the mind alone that preserves what is otherwise an un-preservable instant and turns it into a potentially inhabitable narrative.

Even defining 'the moment' is nigh on impossible. A nanosecond is too fast to experience. A larger split second is not. But how long does a moment have to be, and received with what degree of intensity, to feel significant, to impact the wider span of our lives? Length and depth are inseparable to a perception or sense of the real.

Viewed another way, we do not live in a series of things called 'moments' at all, but rather in a continuous, immeasurable presentness. While, as we say, "the occasion has passed", it is inseparably moulded into an unfolding time-and-space fabric felt in a here-and-now which is ever moving and ever present.

So if "the moment", any moment we experience, was not there we

---

1 'At the Mid Hour of Night', by Thomas Moore, was first published in 1813 in *Irish Melodies* (1807–34), and later anthologised in *Poetry of Thomas Moore* (Macmillan, 1903), edited by C. Litton Falkiner.

would experience a rupture, would we not? Not really. What has *not* happened does not tear the seemingly unified cloth of present, past and future. But a possibility, not even a probability (something that has not yet happened, and still may not), can nevertheless be pregnant with potential and a courier of meaning, even in its non-state. This is because the mind can imagine or anticipate it – again, in the moment.

> *This is the present.*
> *For you. For me it is*
> *the past. And for*
> *someone else it is*
> *the future.*
>
> *Everything has the capacity to hold or embody*
> *memory.*[2]

Beyond Receding Physics and Metaphysics

This ties in with some of the latest postulations in theoretical physics, which question the previously taken-for-granted fundamental nature of spacetime, and ask whether it even 'really' exists, or whether it is an illusion. Perhaps we are filling in the gaps with our mind's eye, or being dreamed ourselves by a larger consciousness? At the same time, according to a certain block view of the universe, what has receded into the past has not necessarily disappeared completely, while what will emerge may already be in existence. Do agents and their agency 'move through' time and space, as they speak and act, or does agency create the temporal and the spatial, and the continuum appearing around them?

The mysteries and uncertainties of time examined from the overlapping observations and proposals of physics and metaphysics may indeed boggle the mind. But the more truly extraordinary thing, which we abide in so ordinarily that we rarely even stop to notice, is our own stretched-out 'living in the moment' as a constant, uninterrupted human experience: one that feels entirely

---

2 This poem, written in November 2024, is entitled '(Fugit)ive'.

PART ONE: Living Beyond Our Moments

substantial, but which (as soon as we think about it) has already slipped away. It is our remembering, individually and collectively, which holds the fabric of experience together, or rather makes it feel like a tellable wholeness.

This wholeness, or unity, is fundamental to human life and human experience. Again, we are largely unconscious of it, while being wholly dependent upon it, like a sea creature in the river or ocean. As Llewellyn Vaughan-Lee says: "Oneness is not a metaphysical idea but something so simple and ordinary. It is in every breath, in the wing-beat of every butterfly, in every piece of garbage left in the city streets. This oneness is life, life no longer experienced solely through the fragmented vision of the ego, but known within the heart, felt in the soul. In this oneness life celebrates itself and its divine origin."

The Cult and Culture of 'Momentariness'

But how do we navigate this oneness, this garment of moments we call a life? There is a kind of culturally fixated post-modernism which is all about living with the ecstatic surface of the time being. Then there is an ever-resurgent modernism that seeks to reshape what is there into something different and malleable, or into instrumentalisable shapes. And there is also a solidly traditioned, pre-modern instinct towards searching for depths, for what is not manifest, for what lies beneath or ahead of the moment and animates everything that is.[3]

We may say there is no depth, because we are looking at the surface; or because we find we can remould what is manifest. Equally, we may dismiss the significance of the surface as ephemeral, because we are currently digging deep beneath it or repainting and reconstituting it. The experienceable truth, however, is that there

---

3 An emerging discourse around 'metamodernism', for want of a much better word (perhaps poetry can help?), is seeking to repair the rupture between these three historically conditioned perspectives, without pretending to stand outside the flow of history. It is more about receiving it all, though not uncritically or without continuing reform.

is no depth without surface, and no surface without depth, definitially. This is so just as there is no surface and no depth which cannot finally be altered, reshaped, refigured or transfigured. There is instead a wholeness partially available to consciousness which makes the present moment possible and provides the structure, data and continuous awareness needed to sustain it, even as it is fluidly replaced.

'The moment', in essence, is not chronological, it is existential. In approaching momentariness, what matters most is not measurement but metaphor. This is something inherent in poetry, and in the poetic approach to life. Our true existence is not seconds slipping away (though they do), but colour, sound, feeling, momentum, expression, hope, joy, wisdom. The rushing wind and the roaring waves. The connected thought and the driven engine. All of these require consciousness, which is fully congruent with physical brain states, but not finally reducible to them[4] without eliminating them altogether.[5]

Consciousness entails us being conscious of being conscious. Reflexivity. A primordial reality. Poetry (and music) is, in part, what emerges from the symbolic structure of subjectivity.

With and Beyond the Moment: Saturation or Narrative?

What most often stops us living in the moment is saturation, which is a huge feature of culture and media right now, with far more to come via Artificial Intelligence, and especially self-generating AI. Digital communication is about 'the attention economy', rapid turnover of messages and adverts, flashpoint messaging, and

---

4   David Bentley Hart, *All Things Are Full of Gods: The Mysteries of Mind and Life* (Yale University Press, 2024).
5   Eliminative physicalists, like the late Daniel Dennett, at least have the honesty to admit this, absurd though it is. Ultimately, all fully reductive physicalism has to deny the existence of consciousness as anything other than an illusion, thus rendering every aspect of our experience, including the positing of this idea, illusory. The alternative to reductive physicalism or reductive idealism is some kind of differentiated monism which sees consciousness as foundational, but recognises that not all *is* consciousness, even if all that is can only be conceived *through* consciousness.

constant distraction. The amount of information seeping into people's lives is almost overwhelming. In the process, through Alexa and many other ways, mind is being trained to consume images, pitches, commentary, sights and sounds voraciously; to be leaping to the next thing, and the thing after that, before what is currently claiming attention can achieve proper focus.

Digital dieting and foreswearing multitasking aside, the real alternative to saturation is the description, discrimination, selection and ordering involved in the process of forming and feeding narrative – a story, or set of stories, within which moments combine and cohere. In advanced capitalism, the consumer narrative is king, because so many of the centres of profit are located in buying more and more, whatever the cost to community, human solidarity, animal kindness and the nurturing of the earth.

Literature, poetry, sculpture, painting, storytelling and music are major carriers of narrative – though each is also prey to being reduced to mere glitter and entertainment. The difference between joy and mere happiness is that the former requires investment and commitment to "serious places on serious earth", whereas the latter tends to be about a series of satisfying events from different components.

Narrative as Liturgy, and Liturgy as Life

Christian liturgy in both the Western and Eastern traditions, or in newer forms like those evolved through the Iona Community, is a classic example of how narratives develop and shape us, when practised and understood well. It brings together poetic language, movement, song and drama to present a succession of scenes in which the participants are invited to locate themselves in relation to an unfolding picture of a world given in creativity, marred, restored and perfected. The focus is Christ, who brings authentic humanity and divinity together, undergoes the suffering and tragedy of existence, and opens a path to life renewed and shared in defiance of all attempts to divide and rule by the forces of earthly domination and empire. Eucharist is an act of *anamnesis*, by which

Beyond Our Means

the past lives on and changes our present and future.

Among the actions at the centre of liturgy ("the work of the people") is gathering around a table and sharing equally[6] in bread, the stuff of life, and wine, the liquid of joy, emerging from the ingested symbolism of flesh and blood. There is so much going on here, it is difficult to summarise. What we have in this ritual is a succession of moments which are more than the sum of their parts, and which bring us together as part of a communal journey characterised by a shared ethos and telos.

This is a deeply layered example of living beyond our moments by integrating them, rather than being pulled away from them. In an age where many (not least the religious institutions themselves) have lost touch with this, and in some cases have become poor relations of the entertainment industry, it is through art that some of what is offered in liturgical expression can be retained, reflected and universalised. Correspondingly, the challenge to both religious and non-religious communities of affiliation and ethical transformation is to make far better and more definitive, imaginative use of the arts, as happened in previous eras and centuries.

Ritual and Symbol in and Beyond the Moment

> *Amora*
> *It's right here*
> *a dragonfly, the Shard*
> *A wild, profane blast*
> *(may cause feelings of joy)*
> *One day is enough*
> *to remember.*[7]

Ritual and symbol, conventionally spiritual and otherwise, are

---

6 The communism of communion, and the arts as evocation, celebration and resistance, are all ideas that feature to a degree in my forthcoming book. Simon Barrow, *Against the Religion of Power: Telling a Different Christian Story* (Ekklesia Publishing, 2025).

7 My poem here is entitled 'Foundling'. It was written after I met fellow poet Kevin Scully recently, and is a found poem. All its key elements are lines from advertisements on the London underground. Turning saturation into narrative.

ways in which meaning is given to particular moments of our lives, not least rites of passage. An example is the wedding ceremony. This is a particular, time-bound event which can embody and embrace the much larger commitment of marriage. But if the marital ritual and celebration is to have meaning, we need to live out of it and beyond it in order to invest that significance within it. This perhaps echoes back to the paradoxes of time (in particular, the mutual inhering of past, present and future, in spite of their apparent separation) which I explored at the beginning of this essay.[8]

The great classicist Stefano Rebeggiani points out that, once in Paradise, Dante's body moves in a time dimension separate from the shades around him. Here is a kind of temporal wormhole, the point of which is to show us that, in this life, time is of real weight and urgency.[9]

There are many other ways to explore the theme of learning simultaneously to live in the moment while figuring out how to proceed from it fruitfully. The chronological event becomes something that can be explored through the recording processes that poetry, music and other artistic media offer, in order to work on how it is that we look in the light of what it is that we are searching for. By love for love, through peaceful means in the quest for peace, et cetera. Means and ends are joined productively when "the moment", whatever it is, can be received reverentially and prospectively. This requires learning, unlearning, restraint and adaptation. It also requires seeing differently.

One poem in the next section (so beyond the moment here) illustrates this well, I have realised. 'Shot Sage Blue Marilyn (Reframed)' is about how fresh sight un-masks and frees the person and the image from appropriation.[10] In the meantime, we must never for-

---

8 As T. S. Eliot puts it, in the opening lines of 'Burnt Norton' (*Four Quartets*, Faber & Faber, 1944): "Time present and time past / Are both perhaps present in time future / And time future contained in time past."
9 I am grateful to Jason Blakely for pointing this out. See Dante Alighieri, *The Divine Comedy* (1321), of which the third part is 'Paradiso'.
10 I was incredibly disappointed to discover how commercialised 'Marilyn: The

get – again anticipating what is to come – that 'We Have Now.' The time of now will, we can be sure, pass remarkably quickly. Through photos, records and a variety of crafts we can retain some memories of the moment, but never capture it. Holding on is not the point. The point is not to miss the moment, or its significance, or its endless reverberations in our lives. That is the beyond in our midst, the eternal glimpsed within the temporal.

Only time can know
Whether the words and gestures
That pass between us
Will abide beyond the moment.

Only time can show.[11]

Exhibition', which ran at the Arches, London Bridge, from October 2024, was. Its promotion suggested that it was trying to move beyond imprisoning images. Its form and the pricing did the opposite. This is a good example of how we can lose the authenticity of the moment as we try to saturate and exploit it.
11   This poem is entitled 'Quantum'.

I
UNPROSAIC

A poem
    is the longest way
       of speaking
the fewest words
    into truth.

———

For Kevin Scully (and all the other poets in my life)

We must learn to listen between the lines. – Anna Deavere Smith

Among other things (some of which are discussed elsewhere in this collection) poetry is inherently a language of intensification and excess. It presses the possibility of meaning with as much economy as elegance or rhythm will allow, and then takes the lid off, such that it can overflow into our lives and change them, if we so will.

The idea that prose must necessarily lack imagination, creativity or originality is one I obviously wish to resist – though without pretending that my own proseifying contains enough of these three elements absent of contrivance. Nonetheless, this is what the word 'prosaic' has come to mean in popular parlance. It signifies "merely" the everyday, the commonplace and the unromantic. As if those were lesser, less worthy, or less complex.

Correspondingly, I would demur from the notion that the poetic cannot or should not be plain and ordinary, as is clearly the case with the 14 words that comprise this verse. Admittedly, they also embrace the paradox that true economy requires enormous resources. That is where verbal density, alchemy and flexibility come to bear. Poetry at its most potent condenses language without truncating meaning. It opens the doors of semantic possibility wide open precisely through its refusal of hasty or easy resolution.

So what of truthfulness? A friend of mine, introducing a course about hermeneutics, once wryly observed that any given text will carry a host of possible interpretations. But it is important to recognise that some of them are still wrong. Since Pilate asked his most famous question, 'What is truth?', and well before no doubt, we have been begging this issue. But just as the everyday excesses of speech-in-practice give the lie to the absurdly reductionist notion that language *per se* is a system of determined behaviour reducible to patterns of stimulus and response (the incoherence of which is amply demonstrated by Rowan Williams in his demanding book *The Edge of Words*), so the pursuit of truth requires a knowing and deliberate sensitivity to the world, the self, the other; plus a moral relation between the three which surpasses the analytical.

As Anna Deavere Smith says in *Talk to Me: Listening Between the Lines:* "Our ability to create reality, by creating fictions with language, should not be abused. The abuse is called lying. Perhaps we understand the precariousness of our situation. We as linguistic animals. At the very least language is currency as we create 'reality'. To abuse language, to lie, is to fray reality, to tatter it."

The world as a set of conscious, responsible and responsive relations is rendered sensible by metaphor more than measurement, though we need both. The difficulty is that the former takes time and attention, while the latter appears deceptively quick and decisive. But it is rarely so simple as that. This is where the different kind of economy generated by poetry can help, among others, natural and social scientists. They will recognise, perhaps more readily than many politicians and advertisers, that a "post-truth" world cannot ultimately be a liveable one.

There is, of course, a correlation of sorts between this poem and 'Unfolding'. Aside from these two, you will discover four other "un" poems throughout this collection: '(Un)quiet Heart', 'Unnaming', 'Unspent' and 'Unwounding'. All contribute, I hope, to an expanding consideration of the relationship between the creative uses of language, our passionate dispositions of living, and our aspirations to sustaining truth-telling across different realms of discourse. Then there is 'Before Words'…

II

FOUND

Four twirls of coloured wool
blue, yellow, red and orange
entwined around bracken and
strung out across the concrete floor
Feather light and story deep
Abandoned yet found
Unforced art
telling you to take your time
Drawing attention to
the slowness of nature
while all else in your culture
says 'hurry'.

These strands conjure a forest
as I take them gently
in my hand and place them first upon
the gate, then a crack in the wall.
Tomorrow they will be gone
but today they are turning
eternity within my palm
Beckoning attention and detouring
the path away from all those
worries that flood the mind
Handing back time to the
weary traveller.

———

For Elspeth Murray and Richard Medrington

I am out with lanterns, looking for myself. – Emily Dickinson

In the late Summer of 2023 I began to take regular walks around Leith Links, the capacious green space less than a quarter of a mile away from where I live. The perimeter walk is a mile and a half. It takes me around 30 minutes, which can seem like half a day when I am in the right mood, or a mere scraping from an hour when I am not.

For most of my life I have been what I sometimes jokingly refer to as an 'urban rat' – someone habitually at home within those ever-sprawling city limits. I am attracted to cacophonous sounds and bright lights, to the bustle of gloriously mixed humanity, to the constant stimulation, the distractions, the local conveniences of cafes, bars and shops, to the sun dipping and rising over a cluttered horizon.

Greenspace is both inviting and daunting for me. The approximation of silence gives time to reflect, but reflection lets the mind's confusions loose. There are fewer souls, but room to be people. So what and who are we are, and why are we so permanently preoccupied? Pathways threaded between the trees scatter the light and give way to shadows, particularly on the cusp of Autumn. My poem 'Found' is about the small, insignificant things which claim attention when attention is freed from all that claims to be, well, important. But probably isn't.

Those coloured twirls of wool were found on the floor by a local school. They went into my pocket and became the living poem for me, an inviting world within a world. The next day I returned them to the spot they had fallen to. What remains is a photograph. I could tell you the exact day and time if you wanted to know. But it does not matter.

The point seems to be this… It is so difficult to slow down if you try, or to pay attention if you strain. Some people can do it in prayer or meditation, disciplines of the spirit. I need little strands of aimless hope to guide me in the direction of noticing.

I cannot recall what else I did that day. It was probably something measurable, something to be ticked off a to-do list. Nothing, however, could possibly have been more significant or transforming than those fibre fragments.

III
WORDCRAFT

Practising poetry
    a dreg booze outlaw craft
Pulling ideas beyond the seamed sky
Bluerending them across every fate fused border

Do not hold back
    from the breaking riverflow
Aglow with sparkling frond and feeling
Thundering new names towards their violent birth

From the cage floor
    horizons flood in fallow
Conjuring a freedomful wilderness
Wordhurled like boulders ejected from fiery heaven

———

For Beth Cross

> *Time held me green and dying / Though I sang
> in my chains like the sea.* – Dylan Thomas

Ideas are like butterflies. They appear and disappear in a moment: joyously free, yet intimately connected. If you try to grasp or possess them, they will evade you. If you do not take notice of them in the moment, they will be gone – perhaps returning, but more likely disappearing. In the right environment butterflies (and words) are plentiful, colourful, magical and delightful. But if you neglect to tend their habitat you risk thinning them, losing them, even poisoning them.

Few poets in the western tradition were as alive and responsive to the butterfly-likeness of words than Dylan Thomas. In fact I can think of none that quite match him. Read, as but one example, his effervescent 'Fern Hill', capturing the innocence and overwhelming joy of youthful life on his aunt's farm, yet with experience and suffering in every shadow.

This was the single work that converted me early in life to "the poetic sensibility" – not because I fully understood it (I surely did not), but because it took me on a journey that was not my own, yet which would somehow become a part of me. Dylan Thomas threw words into the air and covered them in a rainbow of colours and shades. When they returned to earth those words continued to dance, weaving in and out of sight, transporting us to a meadow of enchantment – one laced with darkness and death, but finally knitted together by sheer, unrestrained being.

Here is verse brimming with intense lyrical language and rich metaphorical description. It overflows with the excitement and joy of a child playing outside and feeling an unaffected harmony with nature, yet is deeply aware of the pain of its steady loss. As in 'Fern Hill', there is a hymn-like, liturgical quality to so much of Thomas's poetry, without its confining churchification. Tellingly, the last two lines of a poem about unbounded youthful joy concern death, but their awful beauty opens the heart to life. As Homer says in *The Iliad*: "Everything is more beautiful because we are doomed. You will never be lovelier than you are now… [You] will never be here again."

So, yes, 'Wordcraft' is an inadequate homage to Dylan Thomas. When I read it in public for the first time, I made the light-hearted (but totally serious) remark that one should never seek to emulate his work, for two reasons. He was a genius, and he was demented. Uncopiable in his ecstatic butterfly imagination, but also broken in both creative and tragic ways. The cracks are truly where the light gets in.

"Dreg booze" is actually via Seamus Heaney, another word-alchemist borne of nature. Thomas once referred to his craft as a "sullen art". But he was also an outlaw to polite sensibility, transgressing borders of meaning, creating as well as employing words – as I have done here ("bluerending", "wordhurled", which I will leave to the readerly imagination at this point) – and tearing the fabric of naming from its safer anchors in modernism, romanticism, symbolism or any other readily classifiable literary movement or style. (Somewhat in that vein, though entirely tangentially, "Riverflow" draws on genre-defying anarchic folk-punk songsmiths The Levellers, experienced some years ago at the Brixton Academy.)

Death came, but had no dominion. Thank you, Dylan.

IV

BLUE MOUNTAINS

A gauze of frost stretches across the grass
As we tender tread its crisp, chlorophyl blades
Not wanting to fracture morning
Or break a fragile silence.

If you listen carefully
You can hear the mountains speak.
Pools and streams dappled on their face
Etched in folds of craggy stone.

Now the peaks seem almost subdued.
Blue, vast and vertiginous.
So sink slowly into their dizzy foothills.
Do not let this scattering beauty pass.

For Fiona Jamieson, Alison Cobb, Adey Grummet and Deidre Brock

Beauty is its own excuse for being. – Ralph Waldo Emerson

So far, I have made two trips to Australia, in 1988 and 1990. That is some 35 years ago as I write. Whatever happened to the lifetime in between?

The Blue Mountains form a rugged region west of Sydney in New South Wales. Its dramatic scenery comprises ascending foothills, soaring sandstone ridges, vertiginous cliffs, waterfalls, pools, eucalyptus forests and a series of small villages dotted with guesthouses, galleries and gardens. There are bushwalking trails, too. Echo Point affords views of the storied Three Sisters sandstone rock formation. Magic lies in those hills. They are poetry in stasis, though there is plenty of movement in them. Just not the kind you can ever stay long enough to see.

The blueness of the mountains is of course a feature of the mind, an inference of light playing over those hard and porous surfaces according to the time of day. It is also a function of imagination and an eliding of memories, senses and impressions. The mental sediment of the ages. We make up the world we gaze upon, and it makes us up too. This poem is as much about the interior world as the exterior one, though it most obviously appears to be about the latter.

Here lies a waiting beauty that cannot be lost. The inspiration to write 'Blue Mountains' came not from recollection or trekking (I am good at the former, and terrible at the latter!), but from a few words in a piece of writing by David Bentley Hart which I cannot now find.[1] I am sure I have borrowed other ideas and observations along the way. His turns of phrase are so often glimpses of eternity, an aesthetic of forever. Then, technically, the moment has passed. But not without moral effect.

The colour blue, so it is said, can signify open spaces, freedom, intuition, imagination, inspiration and sensitivity. Here it is rocky

---

[1] David Bentley Hart's *Leaves in the Wind* Substack is at: https://davidbentleyhart.substack.com

and sinuous, joining the sky to the sea in one continuous and inviting whole, but with no loss of variety or possibility. Silence is fragile and precious beyond words. Even the words of a poem.

V
(UN)QUIET HEART

At the far end of experience
    lies the innocence of wisdom, hidden
A fugitive presence
    mostly forgotten
  by the unquiet heart.

Here is something motionless
    untaxed by forethought
Existing between separated dreams
  day-blind starlit moments
    unfolding repair and reprieve.

So how will the ungiven gift fall?
Slowly, like a crowded moon
    toying with the limits of possibility
  Wise only to an open hand
    visible in the shadows.

Now press against those knowledge branches
    until something solid snaps.
Prophesying that political ends
    as sad remains shall die.
  Suffused, brightened, inexplicable.

For Bonnie Evans-Hills

> *Sit down. Be quiet. You must depend upon affection,*
> *reading, knowledge, skill.* – Wendell Berry

Although its subject and focus is rather different, my poem '(Un) Quiet Heart' in some ways emerged in response to Wendell Berry's 'How to Be a Poet (to remind myself)', which I had re-read a few weeks earlier. At that point I had the title for my own verse – which often comes first, or early, for me – and a few other sketchy ideas or phrases.

Reflecting back, maybe the choice to employ brackets was also subconsciously influenced by Berry's. Though my use of this device, which also occurs in other parts of this collection, was more consciously interventionist. It directly contrasts and questions the framing image of the poem. There is, deliberately, no definite or indefinite article here.

So is the starting point a heart that is at peace, or in turmoil, or ambiguous, or oscillating between the two? The answer will partly be to do with how we are disposed in the moment and in the situation, whoever we are and whatever it is. It may also be to do with how we are conditioned in allowing memory, vision and personal priorities to influence our engagement with the world, or how much those things get submerged in the inner and outer turmoil.

At one point in his poem,[1] Berry powerfully invokes patience as something that can grow with age. For "patience joins time to eternity". There is a double sense to this. The long view may indeed connect the temporal to something abiding. Equally, time eventually elides with passing, with death. The two trajectories are, in a certain way, inseparable. To truly live, there must be an acknowledgement of dying in such a way that allows some things to come alive and other things to dissolve or disappear.

My own way of gesturing in this direction concerns openness and letting go. Which is what the truly quiet heart may hope to

---

[1] *Poetry* magazine (Poetry Foundation, 2001). https://www.poetryfoundation.org/poetrymagazine/poems/41087/how-to-be-a-poet

achieve. It feels to me that there is a connection between the ways patience operates in and beyond time, and the "innocence of wisdom" at "the far end of experience". What I am striving for here, and in other parts of this poem, is a recognition that to be wise is not to be mired in complexity, ever-looking for a clever way of joining things up or making sense of them. It is about recognising the deep simplicity of living well and living a good life. This is something that runs to the core of Wendell Berry's work.

How do we begin gather or recover that original, subliminal, hidden or subconscious wisdom (take your pick)? The French philosopher Paul Ricœur, with whom my wife briefly worked at one point, wrote extensively about the cultivation of a 'second naïveté'.[2] It was one of the many ways that he sought to bring phenomenology and hermeneutics into creative conversation, and to explore the power of symbolic language in cultivating self-understanding.

What he meant, in essence, is that we need to move beyond "the desert of criticism", not by abandoning our critical faculties but by looking for what underpins the worlds of functional reason, technocratic aspiration, and political manoeuvring. Which brings me directly to "political ends as sad remains shall die" (verse four). This is a memorable line borrowed from the definitive 1972 album *Close to the Edge*, by the progressive rock band Yes, about whom I have written elsewhere.[3] There are shades of Hermann Hesse here.

As someone deeply involved in politics for the purposes of peace, justice and ecological sustainability over many years, I could not wish more deeply for the rightful end of 'the political' – by which I mean the power of love finally overcoming the love of power. It will not happen in my lifetime or yours, but without conceiving and acting in the light of its possibility, humanity is doomed.

We most surely need a quietude which is not simply restfulness,

---

[2] Mark Linsenmayer, 'Ricoeur on the "Second Naïveté". 29 March 2015. https://partiallyexaminedlife.com/2015/03/29/ricoeur-on-the-second-naivete/
[3] Simon Barrow, *Solid Mental Grace: Listening to the Music of Yes* (Cultured Llama, 2018).

but a patient vigilance rooted in those dispositions of the heart which are so easily drowned out by the grind of daily existence and the magnitude of the challenges our world faces.

First, make a place to sit down.

VI

GONEBYE

Every loss
is a strange angel
tugging at your soul
bidding you to
let the sun pass
weaving light
in and out of sable spaces
holding fragile
your memories
to the counting fingers
slow in the clock
sand-driven
at the small edge of
farewell.

For David Wostenholme (and in memory of Andrew Morgan)

> *We are put on earth a little space that we may learn*
> *to bear the beams of love.* – William Blake

As we age, so our palpable sense of the meaning of loss tends to grow. No matter how vibrant the world around us, and however renewing the continual emergence of new life, the amount of decay and death we encounter personally will increase. This is part of the ecology of life, but the balance of it will shift and so may our attitude. For many, there is a gravitational pull from the oft-quoted "rage, rage against the dying of the light" (Dylan Thomas) towards a certain kind of acceptance. Whether that means peace or resignation may vary, not just between people but among the morphing multitude within each of us.

It is simultaneously true that death is part of life, and life is part of death. If you watch a movie from the 1950s or 1960s it is most likely that everyone appearing before your eyes has now died. Yet the celluloid figures seem more than ghosts. Their memory has transmuted back into the world of the living, so that the sense of separation is blurred, though not dissolved. In a different way, the presence of those we love and who have passed, who have gone-by, embraces both a good-bye (the elision in the title of my poem) and a fare-well (its conclusion). The latter is about their gradual integration and fragmented diffusion within our lives, as well as their recurrence in the unfolding of the narrative of which they are indissolubly part, such that the inevitable fading of one generation becomes an afterglow within the new light of the next.

Within the Christian tradition, 'the communion of the saints' is a particular expression of this sometimes surprising and recursive intimacy of the living and the dead. For Eastern Orthodoxy, those who are with us and those who are beyond us are in a certain sense equally real, and their destiny is *theosis*, incorporation ('incorporealisation') within the realm of divine life.

I vividly remember the powerful instantiation of this in the ritual leading up to the sacrament of baptism at the Church of the Annunciation in Brighton, when I lived there. As the procession moved around the body of the church towards the font, the names of exemplars from the earliest days of Christianity right through to the present were invoked and welcomed into this drama bringing past, present and future together.

Ritual (of this kind and many others, religious and otherwise) is about the creation of community through a sacred combination of movement and narrative. 'Gonebye' hints about both, but in a much more personal sense. Every time I read it, I call to mind different people who continue to make me who I am. Some of those who have stayed with me in the creation of this book are listed in the Acknowledgements. They are testimony to the fact that the absence of presence does not, of itself, enforce the presence of absence.

And difficult though it is – especially in a time of grieving – it can be helpful (for them and for us) to let those we have lost pass through and beyond the light. In doing this we may start to recognise that their shadow is part of the strength of those beams of love through which, William Blake reminds us, we discover what living truly means. We may even find that they return to us in unexpected (and illuminating) ways.

VII

ART FORMS

Strands of human faith and beauty
    weaving pensive filaments
        through a time of questions, heaped
(some asked, many still eluded).

What is on the Playlist of Hope?
    Not a lone voice, but polyphony.
        Not appropriation, but collaboration.
Innumerable chimes, shaping the Big Song.

Now… show me the path towards
    picking up a violin.
(Hundreds heard Menuhin play in Pilton.
But who heeds their ensembled cries?)

Maybe only an incomplete symphony
    can sound out our wounds…
Notes seeded in imperfection,
    by which art orchestrates a future.

———

For Lisa Clark (who said she liked this one), Nicola Benedetti and all the lovely EIF people, and my friends and collaborators on the Edinburgh Music Review, not least Hugh and Christine

> *Music lives and breathes to tell us who we are and what we face.* – Yehudi Menuhin

In August 2023 I was invited to attend three discursive explorations of art and society at the Hub, the interactive base of the Edinburgh International Festival. The first was a conversation on 'Exploring Hope in the Face of Adversity'. It was a wide-ranging exchange focussing on community and the arts – including the impact of class divides and deprivation on access and engagement, culture as a vehicle for social transformation, the saturation of 'entertainment', fighting back against corporate takeover, the impact of government cuts, and the lop-sided economics of the arts under austerity.

It would have been relatively straightforward, I suppose, to write a review or an impassioned op. ed. highlighting untold stories, unfulfilled promises and putative signs of hope. But this would have felt like a stock response from someone who, while also an activist for peace with justice, is unavoidably a member of the commentariat. 'Do we really need more outrage, frustration, hand-wringing and spitting in the wind wrapped up in the desperate search for a bright side?' I asked myself.

Besides, the conversation itself went beyond mere theory and politics, inherently and deeply political though it undoubtedly was. Art is about power, its uses and misuses. No, this was talking directly involved performers, poets, artists and musicians who were and are deeply invested in trying to make a difference through their craft.

Even more importantly, it included the voices of those who have worked with, or witnessed, the impact culture can have on ordinary people's lives – from precious paintings loaned by galleries into homes on a run-down housing scheme, right through to legendary violinist Yehudi Menuhin making an unexpected appearance in Pilton.

Pilton is one of the less flashy parts of Edinburgh – north of Ferry

Road, immediately east of Muirhouse, and southwest of Granton. Its community hall is a far cry from the grandeur of Europe's concert halls and recital rooms. Folk were talking about this for years. Why isn't such an occasion closer to the norm?

In the end, I decided to write a poem rather than an article about this lively (and sometimes thorny) discussion – to respond to artistic endeavour with artistic striving. All the words, ideas and phrases from these four short verses were taken from my event notes.

The bones of the poem were laid down towards the end of the discussion itself, and completed that very evening. Reading it today, it still seems slightly rough-hewn (dare I say clunky?) in places. But it felt right and appropriate not to try to smooth things over and recast them later. This was my raw response to a raw conversation. Parts in search of a whole.

VIII

BEYOND LIKENESS

Entanglement is more than blood
It is lemons dripping in the sun
The uncivilised cat
A three-bridge evening
Once upon our time

The angel of death and purification
An elegy for the sacrificed
Frosty morning, interior lives
The absent body
Awaiting redemption

Wrap your form in mantle grey
Twine, the virtuous form of string
Star inwrought, tested by fire
A hint of blue, nets drying
In the deep divine sky

―――――――

For Carla J. Roth, again and again

Beyond Our Means

> *Integrity and beauty place women at the heart of the story of Scottish art.* – Charlotte Rostek

Beyond and before existence there is silence, 'beyond words'. This is the unnameable reality from which likeness emerges, and around which is seems to coalesce in inchoate moments of longing, desire and decorated perception. The kind we have in relation to painting, sculpture, music, or some such rupture in our usual attempts to pattern and manipulate the world for convenience.

So it was that this poem grew out of a visit to a wonderful exhibition at the Dovecot Studios in Edinburgh on 11 November 2023, my wedding anniversary. The Fleming Collection of Scottish Women Artists features more than 70 paintings, tapestries, engravings, textiles, sculptures and photographs across several galleries, and has been curated in a book and catalogue by Charlotte Rostek. It spans 250 years in total, and covers the complex creative identities of some 45 artists. While women are very much part of the contemporary art scene in Scotland, it is easy to forget that this is only so as a result of years of struggle against indifference and rejection.

Often, when taking in an art show, I will want to read descriptions of a piece and find out about the artists. On other occasions I will not want to be taken away from the impression made upon me of the work itself, leaving aside 'information'. In this series of instances, I became fascinated by the relationship between the paintings or sculptures and their titling. In fact, I became quite preoccupied by the titles in themselves, and the way they connected or disconnected from each other and to different possible thematic ideas.

This poem is therefore built around the titles of some of those pieces of art, weaving colours, concepts, ideas and emotions together across three verses. You can read more about each piece, and view it, in Rostek's book. Here, the words are at play rather differently. Serious play and light-hearted play. The first impression is teasing and surreal. The second is serious, pleading and verging on the apocalyptic. The third moves from waiting (the end of verse two) to the possibility of fulfilment. From grey to blue, from string to paradise, from humour to heaven.

At a Burns Supper, in early 2024, I made the mistake of including this poem as one of three in a short reading. The occasion was one of jollity. I warned that this would be slightly bizarre. It was received with polite puzzlement; including, I suspect, by its dedicatee – though we never talked about it. Maybe we will now. I made the decision to leave out the second verse altogether on the spur of the moment, sensing that it did not fit with the overall mood of the occasion. But what was left hanging on my tongue felt, if not threadbare, somehow inadequate.

There is a lesson here. Let the poem speak fully, even if its presence is a word made strange. It will find its home, when there is one to be found.

IX

WIRED (BLUE GUITAR)

The old man strums alone
with wizen inner sonority.
Unfolding soul shards
Teasing untranquil melody.
Gently tapping towards the world
as it turns on its dark side.

He does not play things as they are.
The notes ring out difference,
reverberating the hollow.
Transforming, juggling,
dreaming lost beauty, buried deep
in those twenty-first century blues.

We are softwired to this music.
Patching the world as we can,
exceeding Bright Heav'ns hymns.
Composing from the tragic minor
notes radiant with stillness
against a hoard of destruction.

―――――――

For Jonathan Crawford, all the guitarists in my life, especially Graeme Stephen, the late Allan Holdsworth (and in memory of Michael Tippett)

> *I cannot bring a world quite round*
> *Although I patch it as I can.* – Wallace Stevens[1]

Various layers of artistic reference are weaved into the simple, three verse structure of this poem. It celebrates an instrument that traverses several of the musical territories I have come to appreciate over the years.[2] But also the unique and particular nature of music as an embodied, physical art and craft in the hands of millions of people. Here the vernacular and the advanced sit side-by-side, complementing and informing one another.

The overarching reference is to Michael Tippett's entrancing sonata, *The Blue Guitar*, written in 1983. This 18-minute piece was commissioned by the virtuoso soloist Julian Bream. Its three movements are evocatively entitled Transforming (medium slow), Dreaming (very slow) and Juggling (fast). They appear directly in the second verse of 'Wired (Blue Guitar)', along with an allusion to the composer's autobiography, *Those Twentieth Century Blues*, published in 1991, itself drawing on the title of the song that features prominently in the 1931 musical 'Cavalcade' by Noël Coward.

Tippett did not play the guitar, and his piano skills were relatively limited. But this enabled him to write for both percussive instruments (far more substantially for the latter) with a freedom, daring and expressiveness through which his own distinctively transcendental voice – whether modernist, lyrical or a combination of the two – was able to find sounds of an almost otherworldly quality. For me, the other composers who are notably oriented towards creating startingly different worlds for the ear are Olivier Messiaen and Toru Takemitsu.

But behind Tippett sit Pablo Picasso and Wallace Stevens, joining him in realising the subject of the blue guitar through the artistic media of painting and poetry respectively. In 1934, Stevens

---

[1] Wallace Stevens, 'The Man with the Blue Guitar', *Poetry: A Magazine of Verse* (May, 1937).
[2] Outside the classical world, the guitarist who will always mean most to me is Allan Holdsworth, who features here in 'Aftersong'.

IX   WIRED (BLUE GUITAR)

attended a Cubist exhibition in Hartford, Connecticut, USA. He was struck by Picasso's painting, 'Old Guitarist', completed in 1904 during his Blue Period. This inspired him to write a thirty-two-stanza poem entitled 'The Man with the Blue Guitar', which in turn provided Tippett with the source of inspiration for his sonata. He was in his late seventies by then, but the piece is full of vigour as well as introspection.[3]

The first verse of my poem imagines an old blues player, perhaps on a porch. It ends with a reference to the first line of Michael Tippett's searing protest against war and injustice, his 1944 oratorio *A Child of Our Time*. There, the chorus mournfully intones that "The world turns on its dark side. It is winter." This forges a further connection with the first line of Stevens' poem. But music does not leave things as they are. It is a process of transmutation (which Tippett talked about on a number of occasions). It starts with the composer, and thereby reaches out to performers, the audience and ultimately the heart of a society through which works of art come into being.

That is the theme of the second verse. The final one deploys the power of music against "a hoard of destruction" via the rousing "Bright Heav'n" in George Frederick Handel's *Ode for Saint Cecilia* and many popular hymns. This is a musical full circle for me, because Handel was my first love as a composer and Tippett the one who has accompanied me more than any other in the past five decades of my life.

---

[3] See Orlando Roman, *Performer's Guide to Michael Tippett's the Blue Guitar* (Florida State University Libraries, 2003).

X
UNNAMING

Do not blurt God aloud
while the world is blooded
　texts load weapons
　　wounds are priested
and hell is re-forged
　in the manacle mind
belief will often bequeath
　its twisted, orphan souls.

Instead go gentle
beyond divining piety
　as to a secret lover
　　hidden in the strainings
of hope wrestled
　faith reset
love enfleshed
　against religion's endless vanities.

―――――――

For survivors, and all who carry the wounds of religion

Beyond Our Means

> *Authoritarianism, with its intolerance for diversity or dissent, is abuse elevated to a social scale.* – Chrissy Stroop

Evil committed in the name of God – though its impact is no greater or less for the label attached to it – remains the most darkly intractable form of wrongdoing. This is because it mistakes for (and justifies as) an ultimate good, something which can only destroy and deprave. It is the intrinsic obverse of what Jesus is recorded as having called "the sin against the Holy Spirit",[1] designating the recovery of wholeness (an act of healing) as an act of malevolence. Strictly on its own terms, he warned, this is unforgivable.

'Unnaming' is my visceral protest against toxic religion, and against the easy invoking of God in a way that ignores or trivialises it. The Latin word *religio* is the origin of our modern English word. It is likely based on the verb *religare*, which means "to re-bind". Our beliefs, whether religious or otherwise, are what we bind and re-bind ourselves to, and most often what we use to bind and re-bind others. What has bound people together in communities of conviction can so easily be manipulated and weaponised into something that constrains, imprisons and kills.

It is important to recognise that this is not solely a "religious problem". Things like ethnonationalism, totalitarianism, fascism, racism, militarism and genocidal hatred have existed both with and without the sanction of religious ideas, ideologies and cults. But it can hardly be denied that attributing prejudice, loathing, victimisation, torture and murder to the divine will gives it a horrifying fixity and incontrovertibility among 'the faithful'.

The infections of unyielding fundamentalism are a particularly dangerous spur towards those varieties of inhumanity – the scapegoating and persecution of refugees, asylum seekers, 'foreigners', migrants, sexual minorities, women, ethnic groups, disabled and sick people, and many others – which break us apart and degrade

---

1 Mark 3:28–30 and Matthew 12:31–32.

us... the opposite of the kind of *religio* that builds healthy community, conscience and compassion.

So what is to be done? Those of us who belong to faith communities have an indelible responsibility to challenge toxicity wherever we see it in our traditions, and to develop life-giving critiques of religious abuse based on life-affirming arguments and practices from deep within our shared lives, texts and rituals.

That is one of the functions of mysticism, alongside liberating theologies of different kinds. People of an authoritarian mindset will often recognise one another across the boundaries of religion, non-religion and anti-religion. This needs to be more and more true of those who wish to nurture human diversity, pluralism and openness, also – so that a universalism of transformative love can confront, contend and disturb the factionalism of resentment or animosity.

Within all of us, what will grow is what we nurture and attend to most. Let it be "hope wrestled, faith reset [and] love enfleshed."

XI

SPIRAL REASONS

The colour of saying
is an empty moon
tendril white
and anchored near the sand.

Wrapping dreams
like feline footsteps
around a blanketing sky.

Tensing kaleidoscopic murmurs
smokeful of adverb
fabric and noumena.

Offering once more to
remake the world.

For all those who take words too far
(You know who you are)

The love of form is a love of endings. – Louise Glück

The colour of saying is the essence of Dylan Thomas. If I had to take one poet's work onto a desert island with me, never to return, it would probably be his. Nard for endlessly pouring out. Something that spills, which cannot but overflow. Its equivalence in music, for me, is Olivier Messiaen – especially the ecstatic *Turangalîla-Symphonie*, about which more at the end of this collection. Suffice to say for present purposes that it is almost too much. Its joy is suffocating. Its lines are tortuous in their beauty. Its pauses, silences and pastel moments are borne as much through pain as prayer.

So it is with Thomas, and so it is with much of the poetry and prose that has moved me most profoundly over the years. Here is an effusion of moonlight breaking through the branches once more. Meaning overflows, possibility is without boundaries, and the collision of ideas and words in chaotically, oddly stabilising. How on earth could I ever convey, let alone capture such a thing? I cannot. You will have to discover it for yourself. Or deem me mad, Perhaps, in reading this, it will be the latter.

So I am not going to begin to discuss here where the images and connections in 'Spiral Reasons' come from, let alone where they might be going. That is not the point. A point is not where to start or continue. You can never arrive at adverb, fabric and noumena from there. And honestly, where else would you want to be?

Also, I cannot love endings.

XII

LIFESIGNS

Ageing is a hazy *Chronus*
(Not one digit yielding another).
You are never merely 'old' or 'young,'
   or oddly in-between.
Time's grave passage
   cannot undo the green spirit
until its duller seductions
   rend desire…
       hearth-hearted.

You are every living moment
   clothed in present flesh
      vibrating with
         wants and tears.
Health holding, fading.
Memories buried in bone,
   loss and longing…
Bodied forth, sinewy wise.
   (And this too shall pass.)

You are not bound to senescence.
You need simply to stretch out
   while you can.
Infirmities come, death stalks.
But you shall remain free
   to inhale fresh-scented tomorrow…
and exhale a rush of
    unstoppable
       dance.

―――――

For LW and all who wish to age without fear

Beyond Our Means

> *Life is not about waiting for the storm to pass, but learning to dance in the rain.* – Vivian Greene

As age advances, time appears to elapse more quickly, and the balances of life shift back and forth. We flourish and fade, gain and lose. There is opportunity and threat, blessing and warning. Elements of each come into view as the rough, eroding sands of *chronos* take their toll: gradually, suddenly, or through some combination of the two.

You may find hints, shadows and echoes of those pairings throughout this poem. At the same time, its verses reflect progress through decline, and the invitation to flourish with conscious determination in the face of mortality. But why is it that some are more able than others to respond to that call, while the pull both ways – to death as to life – is felt deep within all of us? That question can only be resolved, if at all, within "the minute particulars" of life (William Blake).

The cliché that "age is just a number" holds, until the point where it does not. We shall all die. The challenge is about whether we can find ever-new ways of cherishing and investing in life until it slips away, or whether we will allow the dimming of the light to pre-empt us by stealth. Raging against the dying of the light [see also 'Goneby'] is a young emotion. But youth in age is a sign that we have not merely passed through the portal of chronology without experience and learning expanding our horizons, gradually integrating body within the accumulation towards totality that is… soul.

Such integration is far from automatic. As philosopher Jean Klein observes (*I Am*, New Sarum Press, 2021): "There may come a moment in life when the world no longer stimulates us and we feel deeply apathetic, even abandoned. This can motivate us towards the search for our real nature beyond appearances."

Concomitantly, we all have some opportunity to move from *chronos* (time as pure sequence, personified as *Chronus* in pre-Socratic thought) to *kairos* (the right time, the narrative time, the time for being-through-becoming). Let it be.

PART TWO

Living Beyond Our Masks

Love forces us to take off the mask we cannot live within, but fear we cannot live without. – James Baldwin[1]

AT THIS MOMENT in history, authenticity has never been more important, or more compromised by a culture of fakery and distorted forms of masking. By 'authenticity' I do not mean a retreat into the self-regarding portion of our lives (comfortable individualism), or some fantasy about who we are that too easily ignores the disturbances of reality (projected 'identity'). I mean a simple but transformative attention to what is true, what is beautiful, what is serious (enduring) and what is good within our world, within the people around us, and within ourselves. This alone has the potential to pull us back from the brink of both societal collapse and quiet personal despair, and into a liveable future.

The starting point for change is being reconnected to the basics of daily living. What happens in the home, at work, and in our networks of acquaintance matters hugely. It is how we are individuated and socialised. It is the material from which our reality (or our flight from reality) takes place. Large consequences flow from the small choices we make deep within the fabric of our existence. The pebbles are small, but the ripples are wide. They are about how we relate, what we buy, and who and what we choose and care for most, as well as what we fear and wish for underneath and through all that.

---

1 James Baldwin, *The Fire Next Time* (Penguin Modern Classics, 1971).

Who we really are, who other people really are, and how the differences between us can be negotiated fruitfully: these are among the key 'life questions' which rarely appear on any curriculum today. By which I mean not just what happens at school, but in most other gathered or media-conveyed parts of our lives throughout adulthood. Maybe such questions sound far too remote and theoretical? In truth, they are not. They are incredibly practical. At the end of the day, they are about recognising the light and shadow in ourselves,[2] and responding to those closest to us in such a way that what can be built out of those relationships becomes sustainable across the full span of our lifetime.[3]

Who Really Are You?

"All we are not stares back at what we are," says Auden. When I was younger, the two phrases most frequently deployed (often rather brutally and unhelpfully) at points in life where avoidance was going on were "get real" and "get a grip". This was before 'virtual reality' began to subsume the embodied, everyday world. Then the masks we put on each morning started shifting further away from being make-up, self-protection or play. They became part of an increasingly elaborate pattern of disguise designed to monetise ourselves and to avoid the pain or threat of "who we really are". This is not solely a feature of the digital age, but it is undoubtedly the case that social media and living online has accelerated and intensified it.

I put that last phrase "who we really are" in inverted commas above,

---

[2] Light and shadow is specifically Jungian terminology, but can also be used in a broader metaphorical sense which is not necessarily tied to the specifics of C. G. Jung's thought or procedures. It is not a straightforward analogy for good and evil, but is more what is manifest and what is hidden. Though a portion of what is hidden may be there because it tends towards (self)destruction.

[3] Sometimes the threat of the other is being confronted with what Mary Oliver once called "a box of darkness". Says Robin Robertson in *The Shadow's Gift* (Nicolas Hays, 2011): "There is nothing so frightening as facing the darkness within – our inner shadow. We will do almost anything to avoid having to look into the dark places of the soul. And rightly so. The darkness contains much that we mere humans cannot face." We cannot, as T. S. Eliot famously said, face too much reality.

because postmodern sensibility (the age of seductive surfaces and constant distraction) leans heavily into the idea that there is ultimately no "real" at all, only appearances and fabrications. We do not wear masks, we *are* masks. We are our own simulacrum. We become little more than the disguise we choose, and any "more" we allow to be seen is carefully managed and restricted. Almost everyone becomes a client of our image, and clients must never be allowed to be friends, because in seeing past the mask they might accidentally shatter it.

The problem with all this is that the flight from the real self and the real other is not finally possible. If we abandon truth in ourselves and in our relations with other people (through making the purely transactional finally determinative), we collapse in upon ourselves and cause untold damage to those connected to us, often without knowing it.

A key aspect of this (though certainly not the only one – there is power and politics, too) is that abiding question of personal masks and masking. This is the routine artifice we apparently cannot do without, but which can end up gravitating unsuspectingly towards a false world, with a false view of ourselves, a false view of others, and a false idea of contentment if not paradise. Poetry is about probing beyond that falsity, freeing us from the engulfing world of images, and restoring a liberating authenticity to our lives.

Masks, Masking and Unmasking

In Japanese culture it is sometimes said that 'people wear three faces'. One that they show in public, one that applies in family or relationship settings, and a private one known only to themselves. Offering a deliberately chosen 'face' to the world is something that most of us are familiar with. For example, we may be feeling unwell or unhappy inside, yet we decide to smile and say that we are fine when someone asks how we are. Beneath this mask of apparent positivity, however, we choose – or feel compelled – to keep our less comfortable feelings to ourselves.

Similarly, many work and social situations involve (or are felt to require by their commissioners, practitioners or both) certain forms of appearance, behaviour, presentation and language. With varying degrees and combinations of conscious and unconscious decision-making, these adaptations signal that we are going 'into role' for civic, cultural, familial, religious, political, organisational or commercial reasons. If we do not, we will not be 'acceptable'. So we conceal certain attitudes, behaviours and feelings by actively portraying others.

In both psychology and sociology, the term 'masking' is primarily used to indicate a deeper, more systemic process by which an individual will modify or disguise a 'natural' (felt, unforced and instinctual) personality trait in response to strong social pressures, ridicule, or behaviour experienced as intimidating or harassing. This will invariably be influenced by overarching conditioning factors such as a heavily socially controlled upbringing and experiences of rejection or dismissal, as well as direct or indirect emotional, spiritual, physical or sexual abuse. Autistic people also talk of adopting a kind of masking that disguises or re-renders neurodivergent responses to others in ways that conform to neurotypical expectations in public and social settings. This will involve attempting to replicate what others are doing in order to 'fit in'.

A common set of reasons as to why all of us 'mask' routinely and ubiquitously, to one degree or another, would include: gaining social acceptance; seeking to be liked; seeking recognition, praise or acknowledgment; hiding or tempering extreme emotions (excitement, anger, pain, sadness, happiness or fear); disguising a sense of vulnerability or inadequacy; dealing with difficult statements or facts; supressing fear, or seeking to manoeuvre a person or situation to one's favour through different forms of persuasion or – in some cases – manipulation.

These responses embrace a range of conscious, semi-conscious and unconscious behaviours, some of which can become additionally stressful (or worse) in their own right. The 'over-achieving' mask in intensely competitive environments, for example, or the 'macho' mask among men socially, politically and environmentally conditioned to see, seek and perpetuate dominance. This has deep consequences. "As we are, so we see," says William Blake.

Life Beyond the Mask

Masking has also become a voracious industry, we should remember. Advertising exists to persuade us that by buying particular products and consuming in certain ways we can become more popular, sexy, successful, accepted and respected. They are the ladder to 'success' in a status-driven world. Here the masking is itself masked through the manufacture, feeding and amplification of a certain distorted notion of the 'real self' which requires cosmetics, perfumes, cars, gadgets and lifestyle accoutrements in order to be fully actualised.

This 'be who you are' and 'live your best life' sell (but only once you have bought into a particular dream or product) is also frequently linked to a reification of celebrity culture and adoptive 'role models'. It is based in large part on the fabrication of the very norms, standards and desires which these products are then designed to fulfil. At the same time, vast numbers of people are also made reliant on livelihoods and jobs built into the core of a profit system that generates and depends upon such a 'need economy'. This has cyclical processes of constant innovation, growing consumption and built-in obsolesce at its heart.

All of us need masks at some point or other. But we also need to learn how to put them aside, and how (and when) to let go of them altogether. We need to be able to recognise what is truly us and what is adornment or role. Most profoundly, we need to learn that there is nothing to fear in being our true selves. That there is, within our very being, worth, value, dignity and, yes, untamable beauty which – if we allow it to show – will attract similar back from others, confirming its reality in relation rather than in isolation.

For while we are, in an ineluctable sense, alone (no one else can be you), our aloneness is also constructed by, and dependent upon, togetherness. Real freedom is not the choice economy. It is not what can be bought, sold or transacted. It is what is given, often in unseen ways, through the minute particulars of our lives as they encounter, and benefit from, the minute particulars of others.

Masks are ultimately part of theatre. Theatre is a way of standing back from the entanglement and complexity of the world and viewing it differently. All the world is a stage, but we do not forever need to be trapped as actors of the emulating kind. The most challenging and necessary task in life is to be ourselves, beyond role. All else is preparation. It can also be the most difficult task, too. Because so many forces, especially in the quagmire that is advanced capitalism, are trying to capture, exploit or commodify our selves and all selves, so that they will serve the system more compliantly. The answer can only finally be creativity, wherever we are able to find it in our lives. As Paul Levy says:

Unexpressed creativity... is poison to the human psyche. The malady that our species is collectively suffering from is, in essence, the fact that we are not connecting with, mobilizing and expressing our creative nature, which turns against us in self-and-other-destruction.[4]

The poetic imagination shatters our forced illusions and takes us back to what it is to see ourselves and everything around us as unimaginable gift, unpurchasable value, and unending possibility. So, unfold. Take courage to peer out from behind your masks so that you can be fully you once more.

Let us verb
an invisible net
arcing high
into the unrelenting darkness

---

[4] Paul Levy, 'Homage to the Creative Spirit', *Awaken in the Dream* (2013). https://www.awakeninthedream.com/articles/homage-to-the-creative-spirit

PART TWO: Living Beyond Our Masks

> *Nouning daily*
>   *what we cannot parse*
>   *to souls stretched*
>   *far into the heavenscape*[5]

---

5 This poem, one of the first I wrote for this collection and decided to use here, is called 'Unfolding'. See the penultimate, two-word line of this essay.

XIII

BEFORE WORDS

Silence is the place
    where there is nowhere to hide
A quietness between the leaves
    of trees we plant
        but will never sit under.

What you cannot hear
    will tease and conjure presence
Summoning up speechless
    wonder disclosed in the
        unforced rhythms of grace.

———

For Jill Segger, Bernadette Meaden, and Rachel Mann

Beyond Our Means

Tell them, we did not live silent. And we died. Free! – Tara Houska

In meditation or prayer we are often enjoined by those most deeply immersed in these practices, and by wise guides schooled in the art of allowing personal conscience to flow into a wider pool of conscious possibility, to cherish silence. But Quakers are right about this. In the temporal, organic world, silence is a state of mind before it is a state of being. Physically, it does not really exist. No matter how still or quiet you are, a murmur or hint of sound will always be present within this world we share.

In fact, beyond the fairly strict limits of the human capacity to hear – without which much of what currently passes for oral (and therefore aural) communication and music would merge into indefinition and indistinctness – there is a universe of sound which is present only through the mediation of our indirect connections to parts of an animal world that hears more, or perhaps to the unconscious becoming subconscious, and thence the unheard edge of consciousness.

The real meaning of silence is the nothingness out of which we come into being, and into which we eventually pass away, haunting us. The soundless, sightless and senseless presence of the divine – strong for some, fitful, weak or apparently (I use that word cautiously but advisedly) absent for others – is the inner-outer limit present to the time and space in which we live, and move, and have our being. That is a phrase which occurs elsewhere within this collection. It is where the impression of silence arises from, the condition to which we seek to return, the peace in which we long to rest, and the limitless possibility of life risen from cacophony and distortion into the plenitude of creation renewed.

Silence is what happens when the mystical moves outside the merely mysterious and can no longer be grasped or understood. It is the finite echo of infinity. Here is the tantalising experience of experiencelessness (barely a word, for obvious reasons) into which this poem leans. Where it ends up is grace, givenness, gratuity: the opening in the wound of time for which there are finally no words, sounds, or sentences with full-stops. The poetic is life uncontained and inexpressible, but more 'real' than the next breath we take.

Wendell Berry puts it, as often, as well as I could imagine. "Accept what comes from silence. Make the best you can of it. Of the little words that come out of the silence, like prayers prayed back to the one who prays, make a poem that does not disturb the silence from which it came" (*The Selected Poems of Wendell Berry*, Counterpoint, 1999).

In silence, trust is absolute and unnameable, or an ungranulated nothing at all.

XIV
EMBRACING LIGHT

We forsake comfort
    to talk hard and clear
        about what hurts.
To pierce the penumbra
in search of a darkness that is dawn.

But today my heart holds you
    towards the warming rays
        of an unfading Light.
Keep the sun in your heart
A bright leap between minds.

For Lesley Wall

> *Trust your beauty to shine from your eyes and into the souls of those that deserve you.* – Melody Carstairs

Poetry that truly delivers does not usually need too much explanation, though it will invariably depend on context. When well-delivered, it will embrace and shed meaning without artifice. Authenticity is all. So it is in human communication *per se*, and in the kind of personal expression that proves a courier for appropriate concern.

These verses were written two days before someone I truly cared for (though perhaps I was not supposed to) was due to go for a potentially life-changing medical examination. Offering 'thoughts and prayers' seemed, as ever in these situations, so pat and ineffectual. The Quakers have, for me, a much more nuanced and substantial way of saying what needs to be said. "I am holding you in the Light".

The light in question may be, for the beholder, one befitting either a capital L or a lower case one. For me, it is both. There is ineluctable light in wishing someone well, in the attention of a professional consultation, in medicine, and in the search for treatment and resolution. The cracks are where the beams of hope may appear. At the same time, for some of us, there is a larger, more enduring Light there to be discovered. But it is only present if it is there for you. Love is manifested in invitation, never through persuasion.

That, maybe, is where the difficulty resides. How do you show concern without intruding on privacy or reserve? Even a poem may be too much. This one went unremarked. But I know in my heart that the words were and are the right ones. To be able "to talk hard and clear about what hurts" is pure Ernest Hemingway, of course. It is as much a gift as light or love. It is what facing a health challenge, the demands of genuine relating, or the tricky contours of honest conversation (by which we might grow) involves. For some it is too much, too evoking of unresolved trauma or fear. It has its time and place.

XIV EMBRACING LIGHT

Is it *this* time, *this* place? You may never know. But what has been offered in the written word will remain, either to return or to dissolve, as must be. Trust the Light.

XV

WE HAVE NOW

The hole in the fabric
    is so immense.
A palpable, aching absence
    where once there was warmth,
  affection, mischief, companionship
and those routines that pave the day
    and establish that all shall be well
and all manner of things shall be well.

So where is he
    now he is not here?
Still heart deep, in shadows
    that his sight, smell, sound, feel
  and breath cast round a lonelier house
that is the same while never the same again,
    leaping (secretly) to greet you
and in multitude treasurehouse memories.

Death is outside life
    but alters it irrevocably.
Yet and yet, the animus of spirit
    joins us all in a web of shifting
  sea-light love, glinting in those shining eyes,
irreplaceable and forever; expressing the song
    that is always for your heart, even
when it feels in danger of being forgotten.

For Lesley and Ziggy

> *If some people see angels, where others see empty space,*
> *Let them paint angels...* – John Ruskin

Some poems emerge from the seeming happenstance of quite different things you are experiencing, reading and reflecting upon. For me, this is one of them. The impulse came via someone who is dear to me breaking the news that her beloved dog ("he was the world to me") was dead. The look of loss and pain as she spoke affected me very deeply.

It is really important to remind ourselves at moments like this that although we all know what grief is like for us, another's grief is just that – it is not knowable within our own frame. It is theirs, by right. We can never take that away, and nor should we ever try to. Grief is universal, but it is always deeply singular. We can sympathise. We can (of course) truly sorrow with someone we care for on such an occasion of separation. But we cannot "know what it's like" for them. So I am conscious that these verses have to be about bystanding, not inhabiting – unless, by grace, they reach across the divide between souls.

In writing this poem, and during my daily walks on Leith Links, I have been reminded viscerally of just how powerful our relationship with animals is. It is never "only a dog". Indeed, as writer, philosopher and polymath John Ruskin suggests (his words above are courtesy of an epigraph from Salley Vickers' marvellous *Miss Garnet's Angel*, which also inspired the opening lines of the poem, along with Wittgenstein), an animal as much as a person may be the gift of an unexpected messenger. A companion treasured beyond all words (including these) with whom and from whom we experience the unconditional nature of love in its deepest form. This is something that often gets distorted by self-interest within the routine web of human relations. So the loss at the heart of this verse is (in a way, deliberately) multivalent. It could also be a child, a relative, a friend, a neighbour. Maybe, for you, it is.

At the end of the first stanza there is a direct and obvious reference to the "all shall be well" saying attributed in a variety of different

XV WE HAVE NOW

ways to Mother Juliana in her *Revelations of Divine Love*, based on sixteen mystical visions or "shewings" she received in 1373. As I was writing, the BBC Radio 4 'In Our Time' progamme about Julian of Norwich (as she is commonly known) came on, and the words fitted perfectly – not as a trite 'solution' to grief, but as its ultimate context. Only love grieves and remains, paradoxically. T. S. Eliot also cites this line in the third section of 'Little Gidding', the fourth and final section of *Four Quartets*.

'Animus of spirit', in the third verse, is an intimation of what in other contexts has been referred to as *anima mundi* (world soul), the attribution of an intrinsic link between all living beings. For me this connectivity follows from, and ultimately depends upon, an unquenchable, overflowing Love "within which we live, and move, and have our being" (Acts 17.28).

Elements of the first and third stanzas were brought to me in the course of re-reading Joseph Bottum's NPR broadcast 'Living With the Dead' (2014). The final sentiment was inspired by the Norwegian writer and reformer, Arne Garborg: "To love a person is to learn the song that is in their heart, and to sing it to them when they have forgotten." The song, of course, can equally be a canine or other personal presence who, though no longer physically with us, remains accessible through the heart's window. One whose remembrance over time will bring moments of healing despite the unalterable fact of death; one who can rejoin us to the artistic vision and lived hope that communion (mutual indwelling), not separation, may be the final word.

So why 'We Have Now' as the title? Because that is what we mortals do indeed have: a series of torn but precious present moments in which to hold dear all that speaks to us of what it is to love and be loved – both in what and who is here, and in what has passed away but still remains. As Mary Oliver poignantly puts it ('In Blackwater Woods', from *American Primitive*): "To live in this world you must be able to do three things / to love what is mortal / to hold it against your bones knowing your own life depends on it / and, when the time comes to let it go / to let it go."

XVI
YOUR PEOPLE WILL FIND YOU

Choose
   those
      who
Choose you
Put you at ease
Let you breathe
Ask how you are
Hear your stories
Love your depths
Kiss your dreams
Guard your unseen
Spark your passions
Wish your flourishing
Tend your beautiful soul
Honour your dark places
And do not bend you to their need or will.

———

For LMW

Beyond Our Means

> *Tell me every terrible thing you ever did, and*
> *let me love you anyway.* – Edgar Allan Poe

Much of life lapses far too readily into the merely transactional. True friendship is rare. What it rests upon is beyond even reciprocity. It is rooted in a deep recognition of the other as other – apart from, and yet a part, of oneself. The 'ourselves' friendship creates are commitment beyond calculation, even to the point that gain must involve loss.

This verse is almost embarrassingly transparent about what it means to regard and engage another with this kind of love. The punch line is the last one. Is it truly possible to dispossess oneself of need in relation to the other? Of course not. The magnetism of the other, not least that aspect of it which is projection (as it will, in part, always be) is transformatory, but can never be wholly egoless. Because we are human. We need to love and be loved. This is healthy. But true friendship, as an aspect of love-finding and soul-making, is about learning to let go of manipulation. It is a letting-be, and a rejoicing in what can be discovered, nourished and grown through that.

As poetry, this verse feels more than a little formulaic to me. But whenever I have read it publicly, it has connected powerfully with someone in a positive way. Maybe the appropriate designation for its form is 'ritual' – a rehearsal within the pageantry of experience of something that helps us re-orientate back to ourselves. The good we discover and sense in poetry is not always detected in its form, but in the life-resonance that occurs within, and also beyond, words on the page. 'Bad' poems (in the technical and artistic sense) can still change lives, and 'good' ones can leave people feeling abandoned.

It has often been said (not least by me, elsewhere in this collection) that poetry stretches language to breaking point and beyond. This is its gift. But with that gift comes wounding. So it us with the heart touched by friendship and love: the unavoidable

XVI YOUR PEOPLE WILL FIND YOU

claim of the other can make a lonely stranger of our wishes, desires and intentions.

This poem will always be a difficult reminder to me of the connection I craved, and in the faltering and failure brought on by that craving, broke. But it can also be an occasion of learning, and perhaps recovering. For you too, maybe. So "come let us be friends, you and I. The world hath her surplus of hatred today" (Sarah Lee Brown Fleming).

XVII

BLUE ADVENT ROSE

The little white rose of Scotland
is dressed in petalfolds of blue,
whispering an unknown elegy.
Nature's cellulose art,
sealed with a satin kiss
on a perfect stolen evening
(before the skies are closed)

It is late August afternoon
in Edinburgh. The festival rose
is given first on Waverley Steps
(Your hair drifting, your body
cradling a moment of pleasure
from this fragile bloom) while
stars fall across the city lights.

The corolla buds will crease
together now, as fresh winter stalks.
I would change anything in my life
to keep this advent beauty close.
But today I sing a soulful song,
(lost on our fragile Blue Dot)
as the world runs still.

Now, Queen of Flowers, if you
asked me to show you
something truly worth seeing,
I would show you… yourself.
You are the wound and the gift
summer (autumn, winter) gave.
"Oh rose, thou art fond."

———

For LMW

> *Before you die, experience the love of a writer, poet or painter.*
> – Soledad Francis

Poems that abide tend to hold their secrets well. Some are there as tokens, often of love or desire. Others are clues, pleas or wishes. Some remain mysterious even to the poet. Others may be begging to be discovered, but probably never will be. What is truly personal only discloses its meaning when it ignites a hidden synergy between writer and reader. Left unpicked, such poetic secrets are like apples in Autumn, "falling all around you in heaps, wasting their sweetness" (Louise Erdrich). In that way, they enrich the dark flavour of earth, seeding life even as they die. Such are the friendships that never come to be, but could have changed our lives.

In truth, 'Blue Advent Rose' is a whole garden of secrets. For a start, it is not one poem but two. Within each of its four verses lurk fleeting lines or phrases from something I wrote privately and gave to the person who deserved it. In the framed form they received it, it remains precious, unique, and will never be published. It came together during a four-week trip to the United States. Though short, it took me a seeming age to compose. It travelled with me in parks, paths and gardens, being written and re-written until it came as close as it could ever be what I really wanted to say. It was a mile off, but smiling.

This was the single piece of unplanned creativity that rekindled my passion for producing poetry. It happened after many years, following several earlier attempts (which I was wise enough to let languish four decades ago). The person who sparked my inspiration is someone who, as I write this, is sadly no longer in touch. Whether it still sits on an office desk, and whether that is the end of the connection, I have no idea. But its recipient will forever be in my gratitude, my thoughts, and my heart.

However, the story goes on. One August evening in 2023, after my return to Scotland, I quite accidentally fell upon a delicate blue rose while descending Waverley Steps on my way home. It was lying in the gutter, staring at the stars. At the time, I was head-

XVII   BLUE ADVENT ROSE

ing back from a wonderful day at the Edinburgh International Festival, where I had been fortunate enough to share an afternoon stage (conversationally, not musically) with a fine jazz musician, Domo Branch, who had flown over from New York. He went on to perform a mesmerising set with a pianist and bass player he had met just an hour before the gig. It was a magical, unrepeatable fusion – as the best music (and poetry) always is.

The discarded, stem-fractured, coloured bloom (the original was white) was one of a number distributed as part of an art promotion that week. I had actually been given just such a blue rose earlier in the day. But having been distracted, I carelessly mislaid it somewhere along the way. Finding another one not only felt like the undeserved return of a gift, but also took my mind immediately back to the earlier, private poem. Its petals still lie in a glass a few feet away from where I am writing this. They went on to seed the idea of a further, enveloping poem on the cusp of Advent season.

Advent is a time of waiting and hoping in "a world of loss and fire" (Flannery O'Connor, counterpointing T. S Eliot). It is as much a disposition as an observance. The 'little white rose of Scotland' is, of course, the focus of a deep and passionate longing in Hugh MacDiarmid's famous verse – dedicated to collaborator John Gawsworth – which now adorns a sculpted wall on the outside of the Scottish parliament building at Holyrood. By contrast, but also in a strangely symmetrical way, 'a fragile Blue Dot' is adapted from Carl Sagan's existential description of Earth viewed from space. Proximity and distance. Possibly a bridgeless gap, but also the ultimate magic.

Meanwhile, that rose indeed remains the Queen of Flowers for me, with blue being the rune which tenderly wraps its petals. It conjures a never-ending quest for depth, trust, loyalty and sincerity. The final line of the poem is the damage of which William Blake writes ("Oh rose, thou art sick"), but now undone. The wound and the gift reside together. But never lose first sight of the gift, even when you can no longer see it.

All else in these lines must remain layer upon layer of the secret heart. If you think you know, tell me. If you want to know, all you have to do is ask. You know who you are.

XVIII
ACCEPTANCE

Ma ben arde nel core

Unsettling as it may seem
it is our trueself that beguiles.
We are no mannequins
(glittering as those masks are)
Time waltzes in our eyes
as they search for what chimes
Shading behind the screen
dancing around the conversation.
You do not have to
shelter from the gleam as it
grazes your cheeks and
plays fondly to your secret self.
There is no place to hide
in gentle wishes and tender verses
that turn upon a twilight
and melt all stone to dust.
Catch the rain in your furrows
They tendfast gratitude
in so many words, dreams, hopes
and shared kindnesses.

———

For LMW

We contain multitudes. – Sarah Henstra

Within our personhood are many personas, possibilities and contradictions. In some cases, that can lead down a series of thorny paths that get labelled, *in extremis*, a personality disorder. But in its natural, raw and human sense, it is true (to a greater or lesser extent) of all of us. For a certain kind of artist, poet or musician, arguably more so.

The idea that we are not evenly hewn, but variegated in time and space, in emotional and intellectual makeup, in social and private behaviour, is one explored in Walt Whitman's 'Song of Myself' (section 51) and in the Manual Cinema video commemorating his bicentenary in 2019, 'Multitudes'.

Bob Dylan placed his song 'I Contain Multitudes' as the opening track on his 39th studio album, *Rough and Rowdy Ways* ("a kind of literary folk 'My Way'," observed Mark Beaumont in *NME*), echoing Whitman. And then there is Sarah Henstra's cutely observed novel for young people (Little, Brown & Co., 2020), the title of which is cited above. It concerns two school friends (one a Whitman wannabe) thrown together in old-fashioned weekly correspondence by an English assignment. Ah, those were the days. Or were they?

My poem contains echoes and allusions to all of that, but also has a much more personal resonance. When two multitudes meet, from different backgrounds and life circumstances, there can be surprising, affirming connections – but also equally surprising (and potentially damaging) mistakes and misconnections. Whether what misfired will ever be overcome, I have yet to discover. Sometimes souls align, and on other occasions, for one of those, it was only ever intended as a temporary collision and never transcended that.

Meanwhile, there is a lingering question, raised in all our connecting and misconnecting, and in the depths of the soul that struggles with them. That is what a "true self" might be (even whether it might be), and how it relates to the masks we all wear, some more elaborate and apparently indispensable than others.

This 20-line verse, originally written on an agonising train journey, is prefaced by a line from the fourth book of Monteverdi madrigals (1603). It comprises four two-line stanzas (setting out some universal challenges), and then three four-line ones (addressing a more intimate appeal). Maybe that is a gesture of hope? The final stanza both contrasts and entwines pain and possibility, a frown and a smile. My heart declares a truce.

XIX
UNSPENT

Love is incomplete.
You are mortal and will dissolve to dust.
You must dare passion while time remains.
Reach out to find that wild, untameable soul
    To touch and be touched
        by the body within her body.

———

For LMW

Let my words turn into sparks. – Marge Piercy

The heartland of this verse is the incompleteness of what binds us together, and the ceaseless longing and striving for a mutuality which does not simply dissolve on contact, whether immediate or extended.

Modelled closely around a more pithy verse by Jack Gilbert (to whom, acknowledgements and apologies), its territory is the awkward human (and therefore spiritual) tension between psychophysical lust on the one hand, and passionate but intimate reverence on the other.

We are what we most are in the act of giving and receiving love. We are what we most need and seek to be in being consumed by gift and gifting, rather than in what we can consume at the expense of others.

Celebrating incomplete love while daring to reach out for its fulfilment. This is true passion. Soul connection. Deep eroticism.

As George Bataille points out: "Poetry leads to the same places as all eroticism – to the blending and fusion of separate objects. It leads us to eternity, it leads us to death, and through death to continuity. Poetry is eternity; the sun matched with the sea."[1]

The consumer society has killed genuine passion by training us to believe that we can be satiated by more and more 'stuff'. By encouraging us or accommodating us in treating people as things and things as people. There are whole industries dedicated that deadly exchange in order to sell everything from cars and watches to perfume and sex.

The essence of this transactional culture is the evacuation of meaning and relationship from everything that can be turned into a profitable commodity. All of us, to some extent or other, are caught up in this system of gradual, persistent dehumanisation.

---

[1] George Bataille, *Eroticism* (Marion Boyars, 1974). Translated from the French by Mary Dalwood.

XIX UNSPENT

For most people, it is easier to imagine the end of the world than the end of consumer capitalism.

To be mired in guilt or to cast blame and aspersions towards people whose lives and incomes are dependent upon monetising themselves and others is not the way forward. It is the opposite of what we need. It is projection. Passion beyond possession is rekindled not by judging, but by loving.

The erotic is felt most deeply in creativity and touch which heals, hopes, dares, dreams and desires the fulfilment of the other, and in that the discovery that our own otherness is to be embraced rather than feared.

This happens when we give ourselves freely to what cannot be controlled by our own restricted interests and fantasies. It is about what connects us most deeply. Desire within (and therefore beyond) the neediness of 'wanting'; embodiment within (and therefore beyond) abstract bodies or a 'body count'.

Equally, the carnal is only bereft of the spiritual when we are afraid to be truly present. But the present will pass if we wait for the perfect moment or the perfect person. Do not fear incompleteness. Dare. You may not get another chance. Or another inviting stranger quite like this.

"To touch and be touched". That is so much… more.

XX

SHOT SAGE BLUE MARILYN (REFRAMED)

La Demoiselle d'Hollywood
Lies naked, splintered and masked.
To meet up with the men she loves
She imagines herself in Paris.
A face that immortalizes the centuries
Iridescent skin and shadowed eyes
Staring into
An aching garden of roses
Thin red budding, see-through blue.
The woman stands alone
Singing where there is no other song.

The Birth of Marilyn, Mona Monroe
Acrylic and silk screen on linen
Forty square inches
A thousand emotions and a million shutters
Exhausted, or maybe even alien
Canvas and face cloaked in dust
On whorehole's uncommitted blue
Her smile rendered stale
Flooded with lipstick and
Piercing sweet golden locks.

A deep irony locked within this body
The secret poet, overcome by fame
Cool as a forgotten dream
With no one
Finally there
On the end of her phone.
Perhaps a divine whisper
Behind the masks
Maybe … may be?

For LMW

Beyond Our Means

> *I believe in myself, even my most delicate intangible feelings.*
> -- Marilyn Monroe

In the tawdry, cliché-ridden reportage that dominates the eternal reconstitution of her image, Marilyn Monroe's likeness is repeatedly said to be 'iconic'. Traditionally, an icon is a window onto deeper meaning, its surface being something we are invited to learn to look beyond, rather than stay with. Whereas Marilyn's portrayals are frequently stuck in the ossifying objectification of the male gaze, monetization, and the masks she chose both to advance and protect her elusive, wounded, artistic self.

This free-form poem, with collage elements, is set in three 11-, 10- and 9-line stanzas. It is shaped by found phrases from several sources. At its core, in the second verse, it deconstructs (lines 13 – 21) Andy Warhol's famous 'Shot Sage Blue Marilyn' silkscreen painting (1964). This is one of a series he devised after her tragic death in 1962. It was so-called because performance artist Dorothy Podber presciently fired a bullet through a stack of four of them. Warhol described the retread blue one as 'dead art'. He was right, but that did not stop it being sold for $195,000 in 2022, making it the most expensive twentieth century artwork purchased in a public auction to date. Thankfully, the money went to various good causes. Unlike the proceeds of the Barbie movie.

The first and third verses of the poem invoke Marilyn's remembered and forgotten life and demise, otherwise lost in her 'iconography'. My reframing of 'Shot Sage Blue Marilyn' in verse two cites Benjamin Schmidt's visual critique of the painting (*The Interior Review*, May and December 2022). As with the title of the poem, it also provides a link to the marvellous all-women CNN 'Reframed: Marilyn Monroe' documentary television series -- dethroning the monolithic male fantasy of Marilyn in favour of a vibrant woman brimming with feminism, ideas, sexuality, power… and, we must add, song (lines 10 and 11) and poetry (line 23). On the latter, see Marya E. Gates, 'Marilyn Monroe's Truth Was in Her Poetry' (*Vulture*, 12 October 2022).

The Paris allusion in lines 3 and 4 is evidently ironic (Tara Hanks, 'Made in Paris': Was Marilyn a Secret Francophile? *The Marilyn Report*, 16 July 2022). But the reworked instancing of art by Picasso ('Les Demoiselles d'Avignon', his controversial brothel painting (recast in line 1 against Andy, the real 'whorehole', later in line 18), alongside Botticelli's 'The Birth of Venus' and da Vinci's 'Mona Lisa' (both in line 12), are equally deliberate. They are contrasting (though artfully superior) examples of the way men choose to see, mask, irradiate or frame women.

Meanwhile, the 'garden of roses' (lines 7 – 9) is a reference to the title of artist Dganit Blechner's powerful 3D double-layered image, "emphasizing Monroe's multifacetedness and her hidden inner world in contrast to her public image". It contradicts Warhol powerfully. Marilyn herself produced a delicate, wistful painting of a red rose, auctioned for $78,000 in 2005. 'Behind the Mask of Marilyn Monroe' was a theatre piece performed in Avignon (cf. lines 1,2, 29) on 27 May 2023. "Cool as a forgotten dream" (line 24) is borrowed from Gwendolyn Bennett's haunting 'Moon Tonight'.

The poem's conclusion, built towards the puzzle of the unanswered phone as she lay dying, was sparked for me by re-reading Nicaraguan poet and revolutionary priest Ernesto Cardenal's affective and touching 'Prayer for Marilyn Monroe' (*Apocalypse and Other Poems*, New Directions, 1977) on the occasion, context and circumstances of her death. I was privileged to meet Ernesto briefly in 1985. I was just four years old when Marilyn passed. Both live on, in different but oddly connected ways.

XXI
MYSTIQUE

Perfume and incense
 A cloudy allure
  Falling into that presence

   Hypnotic
    Kenotic
     Erotic

      Love
       Live
        Lose

On the way to, and back from, Northampton

Beyond Our Means

Someone I loved once gave me a box full of darkness. It took me years to understand that this, too, was a gift. – Mary Oliver

Sometimes my poems end with love as the final word. Then again, just as often (perhaps more often; I haven't counted) they end with loss. Which is it to be? In this life both are inextricably intertwined, but in purely mortal terms loss always appears to be the final word – as it is in this verse. To be and not to be. Then again, appearances will be partial. How are we to evaluate what departs from us *sub specie aeternitatis*, in the long view, through the arc of love, with a divine possibility, under the aspect of eternity? With and without you. Present and absent. Prose and poetry.

This verse works as three stanzas of decreasing length. Some of me felt that they fitted better together as one continuous, if brief, poem. In the end I hedged my bets. The nine lines break into three sets of three, with an unsignified *selah* in between, and there is a correspondence between them in two apparently contrasting ways. If you want to discover what 'Mystique' is about, first read it as it stands. Then read lines 1, 4 and 7, followed by 2, 5 and 8, and lastly 3, 6 and 9. Then do that in reverse order. Those configurations are full of intent.

Now you may choose your own arrangement of the first three lines, stacked against one from each of the two succeeding stanzas of three. Randomly if you like, or perhaps with some readerly intent or wish of your own. Maybe simply as an act of discovery. According to my calculations there are 162 possible permutations, including reversals, which would make a very short poem (16 words over 9 lines) into a very long one. Then again, I never was any good at maths, and I have not completed this experiment. One day I might.

I had to tell you this, or you might never have figured it. Then again, perhaps you would. For it means everything and nothing. Which is also what the poem concerns. That and the fleeting presence of the other, the numinous, the beloved, the transcendent.

The message. This is always changing, and always the same.

The erotic is fullness. Kenosis is self-emptying. Hypnosis is some kind of negotiation between the two. Being bound to the moment, yet never fatally suspended within it. Loss is only penultimate if we are held. Love is what holds us, living is what translates that into relationship, letting go is what distinguishes it from possession.

Perfume is about desire. So is incense. Are the two so far apart? Yes and no and somewhere liminal – in the *shekinah*, the forbidden touch, the luring scent. Here is the fleeting yet ever-present nowness of presence. An unbearable likeness of being and being over, altogether. This too is a poem, rightly construed.

Then there is Charles Péguy, the French poet and essayist. He once said that everything begins in *mystique* and ends in a *politique*. I rather think his aim in life was to reverse that process. So is mine.

XXII

ORPHEUS UNTOLD

      Back. Look. Don't.
Many maenad masks
  in and out of time
Rebirthing music from
     Apollonian light
  and the venomed dead oak-nymph.
Eurydice leashed beyond
   our temporal veil
    The secret theatre
of the underworld.
   Ravaged by Aristaeus.
Losing love hurts; keep moving.
     Back. Don't. Look.
   An apparition, the parallax view
    persona, mime and puppet
      Arch upon Arch
  wings, colours, blood, glass, fear
and a dozen more.
Orpheus scored, storied, mythed
 and dreamed
   in a many-scaled modal veneer.
    Dissonance unbound
  an electronic aura
pushing sound into the whirled
   new world. Argonautica Orphica. More
     than (ever) meets the ear.
      The lyric muse groove is
interrupted again and again
   a polyrhythmic continuum.
Black sun vision, the Tree of Sephiroth
   disintegrating Eurydice
     for. ever.

The clanging and clinking of brazen bells
A flying golden carriage, singers
masked against raging, wresting time.
in blue broken images
Don't. Look. Back.

To all musical adventurers (and in memory of Harrison Birtwistle)

XXII ORPHEUS UNTOLD

My lyre must always play. For without music we are nothing. We knead the shapes out of nothing. Tunes out of silence, love out of hate. Music that lasts forever. – Orpheus

Harrison Birtwistle's *The Mask of Orpheus*, with additional electronic music created by Barry Anderson and a libretto from Peter Zinovieff, is perhaps the most significant, ground-breaking opera of the late twentieth century. Premiered by English National Opera (ENO) in 1986 and performed in a concert version at the Royal Festival Hall in 1996, it was not seen on stage again for 33 years until the controversial, dazzling, transfixing ENO revival in 2019.

Birtwistle and Zinovieff present the Orpheus story as a collection of fractured, contradictory myths. Linear time is abandoned. Events are reprised from different perspectives as they are predicted, as they occur, and as they are remembered. The three main protagonists, Orpheus, Euridice and Aristaeus, are each represented by two singers and a dancing mime, conveying – respectively – the person, the myth and the hero. The sequence of arches provides one of its key allegorical tropes. A straightforward synopsis is all but impossible.

The score itself is immense, complex, sinewy, detailed, striking, meticulously structured and punctuated by beautifully eerie electronic interludes. Here is a masterpiece which both utilises and challenges every operatic facility and possibility. Each act has its particular sonic 'aura'. The music does all the heavy lifting, and even in a production as visually gauche as ENO's six years ago, it carries all before it, but without overwhelming the theatrical patterning which is matches and shapes. To borrow Gertrude Stein's phrase, it "describes things without mentioning them".

The form of my poem is itself a kind of verbal drama and ritual. It references (and in a couple of places emulates) the procedure of one of Birtwistle's other signifying compositions, *Secret Theatre*. This draws on *The Mask of Orpheus*, alongside parallel works, in bringing instruments forward for monologues and then grouping them in shifting alliances concerned primarily with melodic, rhythmic or harmonic material.

The first, thirteenth and last lines of 'Orpheus Unmasked' shape the whole and deliberately dismantle the chronology. In reading it, certain patterns occur, recur and fracture. There is present within the bundle of Orpheus narratives that Birtwistle and Zinovieff draw upon, a certain 'mythic pattern' that represents the experience of loss, unconscious yearning, depression, and psychological inflation. I have tried to give voice to those. Beyond that, it is better to leave further exegesis of this poem to the reader.

Inter alia, other adaptations of the myth of Orpheus and Eurydice, created within a decade of this opera, include Woody Allen's dark film *Deconstructing Harry*, and 'Eurydice in the Underworld', a short story by Kathy Acker, written in the last year of her life. But for me it is Harrison Birtwistle and his collaborators who truly bring the possibilities and contradictions in and around Orpheus together, stretching the muse of music to its dramatic limits, kneaded out of silence.

XXIII

CANDY AND DUST

Wisdom strains
   through heat, carnage and folly
Words decay to mental floss
   Terrorised, flattened
     by trivialities.
Laid empty by consumption
   Eaten up
     by nothing.

Only beauty can save us
   from cog-ex-machina
Unconcerned with speed,
   success, wealth,
     celebrity or efficiency.
(So love revolves again,
   magicking the world
     to dust.)

———

For Tom Hurcombe

Art in its purest form is resistance. – Benjamin Hammond Haggarty

Our species (most particularly – but not exclusively – in its white, western, privileged, patriarchal form) is, as the late Neil Postman observed nearly forty years ago, actively engaged in amusing itself to death. The deadly distractions of saturating consumption, the morphing of the arts into mere entertainment, and the blanket televisualisation of literacy were the chief culprits in his disturbing 1987 narrative of collective cultural decline. That was before the rise of digital and social media, all-consuming tech giants, streaming services, 24/7 news, ADHD and AI.

Now we live, simultaneously, in an era of Trumpian (and Johnsonian and Trussian) post-truth politics, hyper-inequality, the rise of a populist, authoritarian right, and a growing gulf between democratic aspirations and technocratic delivery. As we shop away regardless (those of us who do not live on the brink) there is widespread effective denial concerning the realities of global heating, shrinking biodiversity, expanded precision killing capacity, and the trauma experienced by many millions of displaced people worldwide.

Black philosopher, revolutionary Christian and provocative public intellectual Cornel West often reminds us in the course of his talks and lectures that we are all on a short journey from womb to tomb, but that how we choose to spend our few years on this fragile earth can nevertheless make a significant difference. Right now, too much of our existence rests between candy and dust, glitter and gall, trivia and dissolution.

Nevertheless, I am with Dostoevsky and many others in believing that change is most likely to happen when the human soul is illuminated; and that it is in being touched by beauty, above all, that we are set on fire with the love from which the only true revolution can occur. Yes, we need organisation and determination. Anger and desperation can light that flame, too. But unless they are transmuted into something transcending the desire for revenge and the expiation of bitterness in looking to transform

XXIII CANDY AND DUST

the world, what results – within and outwith ourselves – will likely crumble, turn sour, or worse.

This is what the second verse of 'Candy and Dust' is about, though the positive erosion it seeks, in the first instance, is the shrinking of the bigger, better, faster consumer-driven culture. The end point, however, is not magic in the stars, which is mere sparkle. Rather, it is magic in the stardust that is our humanity, scattered a million ways and waiting for the light to touch and transform it.

XXIV

RECONNECTED

Let the wild rumpus start
Imagining worlds we no longer lead, but might.
Restoring endless delights
   to a gash in the soggy moor
Taking down the fences, blocking the drainage ditches.
Rowan, raven, sallow, birch and hawthorn
   growing through stumps of remnant forest
      between porcupine tufts of unpalatable grass.

The land and I are rewilding;
  a dream of wildcat and wolverine roaming free
Let yourself be absorbed into something larger and less tame
  Feral, ferocious, unbroken
The day before me undresses in the wet
  An ancient blue alchemy
I will follow with my still butterfly eye
     a world less circumscribed by fear and greed.

———

For Alastair McIntosh, Chris Hudson, and Fiona Brocklesby

Beyond Our Means

> *We have privileged safety over experience; gained much in doing so, and also lost much.* – George Monbiot

The call of the wild began, unexpectedly, in the bathroom. I had been reflecting on changes in my inner landscape, and that of others, brought about by more regular walks beyond the city limits, or in its green-patch interstices. There it was that I chanced upon George Monbiot's book, *Feral: Rewilding the Land, Sea and Human Life* (Penguin, 2013), fresh on the heels of dipping into the equally apposite *Regenesis: Feeding the World without Devouring the Planet* (Penguin, 2022).

As Gary Fuhrman succinctly expresses it: "Monbiot has the eye of a naturalist, the soul of an adventurer, and the storytelling ability of a good journalist. His descriptions of his own encounters with the wild make for exciting reading." They do indeed. In redrawing our imaginary of 'the countryside', renewing our understanding of what is possible beyond the devastations of industrialisation and agriculture. and re-energising our appetite for change, these books take us back to what is found and what is given in the world.

It is appropriate, therefore, that 'Reconnected' – which is much about the human spirit as its environment – is mostly what gets termed "a found poem". Most of its lines and phrases are taken or adapted from ones found in these books or in comments about them, including various commendations. My art and craft here, such as it is, lies in weaving my own narrative and invitation out of these received elements. It came to be in a wild rush, appropriately enough.

To discover where the various wordpieces come from, and their original contexts, you will need to read *Feral* and *Regenesis*. While you are there, do not miss George Monbiot's latest book with Peter Hutchison, *The Invisible Doctrine: The Secret History of Neoliberalism And How It Came to Control Your Life* (Penguin, 2024). Also Alastair McIntosh's vital *Riders on the Storm: The Climate Crisis and the*

Survival of Being (Birlinn, 2021). They are both about the larger narrative we need to deconstruct, reconstruct, reweave and rewild.

PART THREE

Living Beyond Our Means

You know only unbearable yearning. You have forgotten that the longing itself is the answer to the longing, that in the very crying out for the Holy One, the Holy One is pouring herself into you.
– Mirabai Starr[1]

THE CONCEPT OF 'living beyond our means' has long fascinated me. In common parlance, and particularly in money-related matters, it is what we are firmly taught not to do. As people, as families, as communities, and as a society. Or at least, that is the theory. Even though public finances do not in fact correlate with household ones (a government can commission the creation of credit, you cannot), politicians of different stripes still regularly moralise about not spending more than is in the treasury. Of course, this is quite impossible, and they almost never do it. In fact, the financial system as it currently exists (for good and ill) depends heavily upon lending, borrowing and everything that can be accrued and deployed on that basis.

The way this works under advanced capitalism is that the wealthy gain enormously from sometimes reckless financial speculation, from markets which trade in futures, from getting the state to give them billions, from colonial plunder, and from exploiting the Earth's resources even to the point of catastrophe. The majority, and especially the have-nots, meanwhile, are strictly urged not

---

[1] Mirabai Starr is a bereavement counsellor committed to the practical idea that "embracing mysticism in our everyday is a way of being more alive in the world, an awakening to the interconnectedness between all things." See her book *Ordinary Mysticism* (Collins, 2024).

to spend more than they have, scolded when they do, offered little mercy if things go wrong, and punished when they fall. Living *within* our means in a class society is a class concept. It all finally depends upon who controls the means and the rules, by what (weighted) system of exchange, and to what ends. This is, to a large extent, an artificial construction.

Life is Abundance and Relation

Now let's think about how life actually works organically, and what happens when we want benefit (in far more than material terms) to be shared rather than hoarded. First, in terms of the actual ecology and *oikonomia* of the life that produces and sustains us, our own personal means will always be entirely inadequate. We need each other, we depend upon each other, we are constituted by each other. From the food we eat to the shelter we seek, from the road we travel on to the school we wish to educate us, from the hospital we hope will treat us and to the culture we need to nourish us, we are utterly dependent.

Without our parents we would not even exist. Without our friends we would shrink. Without those who know, do and provide things beyond our ken, we would wither and die. All life is social. All people are persons-in-relation. Learning to recognise, value, nurture those (and many other) dependences together, in a healthy way, is what might be called inter-dependence.

But it is also far beyond even that, if inter-dependence is thought of purely in terms of markets and contracts. It is about living, giving and creating without calculation. It is finally the only way to live a good, positive and fruitful life. But getting to that place of mutual generosity and benefit involves quite a bit of unlearning and relearning, personally, corporately and spiritually.

Learning Liberating Dependence and Gift-giving

The first lesson is that we *are* dependent. We need independence to grow, but complete independence is a myth. The resources we

PART THREE: Living Beyond Our Means

have within ourselves, or the ones we can produce and purchase strictly by ourselves, will never be enough to 'pay' for everything that we gain with and via others throughout life. To learn our history, to stand in front of a great work of art, to be confronted by great architecture, or to listen to a great piece of music is to be enriched by something beyond our capacity or control. Something for which we could never make full recompense. All these are (or ought to be) part of a growing commons which are everybody's inheritance, rigtly perceived.

You can monetise and commodify almost anything, of course. But that is the path towards knowing the price of everything and the value of nothing. If we try to cost everything, we will find that we are in permanent debt. Then we will try to outsource that debt, while at the same time failing to notice that the true debt we have to each other, to our forebears and to the world (if we try to estimate it in terms of possible exchange value) is unpayable. So we need a new way of seeing. Not debt, but gift. How we best proceed, therefore, is by forgiving our debtors in recognition of our own need to have our debts forgiven. That happens when we stop seeing our dependencies as debts and start seeing them as gifts. Then life becomes reciprocity first and foremost. Living beyond our own means alone is simply the way it is, for us and for everyone.

The second lesson involves finding the most appropriate ways, for us, of living, giving, creating and gifting freely. In whatever ways we possibly can. Yes, we have to earn a living, most of us. And, yes, the skewed money-system (within which we struggle, and choke and lose our being) works overtime to make that easy for some and very hard for others. But something as small as a smile freely offered can change lives for the better. If that sounds clichéd, it is because an entire culture of formation within the financialised system wishes it to be so. In order to make a gift economy, a caring economy, a well-being economy rare and difficult, an economy of possession, consumption, ownership, control and accumulation must be the ubiquitous, unquestionable norm.

"A smile or a poem is all very well, but it doesn't pay the bills." True, but in a life well-ordered (that is, ordered towards the good) they are both precious beyond price. By contrast, the anti-gift economy within which we are trapped, and by which we trap others, is precisely what is leading us to social collapse, political turmoil, endless destruction, climate catastrophe – and, as I have noted elsewhere, personal despair and mental anguish.

Beyond Our Means, But Within the Means of the Earth

In order to address the looming ecological disaster and to reverse the vast and unjust inequalities of the present world order, it is of course crucial that the human species learns to live *within* the means of environmental sustainability. However, in order to let go of the greed that prevents this, and to learn to mend or replace a world dominated by the interests of capital, we need to discover all the good, true and beautiful ways we can imagine of living *beyond* our purely private means – interpersonally, socially, artistically, culturally, and spiritually (as well as politically and economically).

It is that renewed human spirit, maybe even among a few at first, which will eventually enable us to reproduce value rather than wealth, to generate sharing rather than hoarding, to allow a spirit of generosity to infect everything we do, say and conceive.

Indeed, the genuine spiritual life (whether it is conceived within or beyond the bounds of 'religion') is always and everywhere about recognising and practising living beyond our own limited resources, and instead letting gifts overflow into and out of our lives. It is the communism within communion. It is about not needing to count the cost, but instead acknowledging with frequent and renewable awe the way our lives are weaved into a world which – despite its deep fractures, failings and flaws – provides all we would ever need to live in harmony, mutuality and generosity as mortal, temporal beings.

Of course, this is far easier practically (but perhaps much more difficult spiritually) for those who have, in material terms, more than enough. Then again, some of the greatest acts of love are shown by those with few if any such resources. This is not in any way to justify material inequality. Quite the reverse. Moving more towards a gift economy in our everyday and corporate lives is about using every means possible to break down the barriers between us (not least those of wealth and power) and to remake the systems we have built with our own hands, and can therefore also demolish and rebuild.

This involves combining, rather than positing as fundamentally antagonistic, the spiritual and the material, the personal and the political. "Bread for my neighbour is a spiritual question", Tolstoy once said – not because he denied the materiality of bread, but because he recognised that in order to deal with the material redistribution of wealth and power that is required to ensure that all get access to bread (and roses), we also need a fundamental change of heart and vision, as well as a plan and capacity to "agitate, educate and organise" towards a better future.

Seeing the Material as Spiritual, and the Spiritual as Material

Rebuilding the earth together, starting together with our own portion, is therefore also about – and fundamentally requires – allowing our "mind-forged manacles" (William Blake) to be gradually (better still, rapidly) dissolved. To discover a materiality of 'enough is enough', while at the same time practising an economy of abundance which is based on so much more than the acquisition of more and more things, for example. Or reforging our economics so that its goals and measurements are to do with what really enables human beings and the planet to flourish, rather than seeing outcomes in terms of ledger profits, stock value, abstract productivity and wealth accumulation.

This means unmasking and rejecting the world as advertised. In much of the world we are surrounded and saturated by messages telling us to buy, consume and lust after something – always a thing – that is bigger, better and more. We rarely recognise it as such, but this is deep spiritual formation. It is the religion of Mammon seeking to enlist us as dependent followers in a damaging and pathological way.

The world as advertised has a strangely distorted ideological underpinning. On the one hand, it tells you that you need more and more stuff. On the other hand, it reminds you that, because you are subject and have to live within your limits materially, you have to give yourself unconditionally to the system. It will then enable you to acquire the means to buy the very things it remorselessly throws in your face, and tells you that you cannot be a fulfilled person without.

The arts – including poetry, music and drama – are among the best ways of resisting the advertising machine, and cultivating alternative ways of seeing the world. That is why they are a threat, why every effort is being made to make them depend on advertisers, and why they are being defunded. As part of that process, they are "valued" only in terms of economic consequence and output. Not as fundamental goods in their own right, irrespective of what they mean in or for a money-driven economy.

As a result, many "creatives" (note the functionalist terminology) find themselves living beyond their means in a literal physical, economic sense. Among the wealthiest economies in the history of humanity, it is increasingly difficult to survive as an artist. Instead, the arts have been turned into "entertainment" – mass pacification that drives towards the lowest common denominators of human response and behaviour, rather than the highest common factors that feed our aspirations and dreams.

To live beyond our means emotionally, relationally and spiritually in this degraded political and economic context is therefore about finding ways of going on writing, playing, painting, sculpting and creating against the tide. For "what matters at this stage is the construction of local forms of community within which civility and the intellectual and moral life can be sustained through the new dark ages which are already upon us."[2]

Living Within and Beyond Our Mortality

Living beyond our means spiritually and creatively also involves recognising and dealing with our mortality differently. It means finding, using and appreciating the strands of flourishing within and outwith those limits that mark our short journeying from womb to tomb. The loss of those with whom our lives have been enmeshed are among the poignant occasions that offer this opportunity and challenge. They provide a measure of where we are on the path away from unhealthy dependence, beyond merely contractual interdependence, and towards those forms of mutual, loving dependence by which we may discover true liberation.[3] In the meantime, we have to negotiate an odd and variable mix of pain and gratitude, tears and smiles, dust and glory.

> *Let the sky cry for you today*
> *Every raindrop a mixed emotion.*
> *Save ones that recall happiness and*
> *Let others gently wash the mud away.*
> *Evermore we travel into emerging Light.*
> *You, and all those you have loved and lost,*
> *Willing a timeless peace to moisten our souls.*[4]

What death teaches us, among other things, is that learning to live beyond our means spiritually and creatively is not about despising what little we have cultivated out of the soil and tools we have

---

2 A sentence from the famous last page of Scottish-American virtue philosopher Alastair McIntyre's *After Virtue* (Duckworth Press, 1981).
3 I am minded of the extended foreword to the English version of Jürgen Moltmann's *Theology and Joy* (SCM Press, 1973), about the relative claims of ethics and aesthetics, written by David E. Jenkins. Here Jenkins observes that dependence is invariably thought of in a pathological way post-Freud. But he posits that what would be truly freeing for our human condition would be a liberating dependence, incorporating elements of both independence and interdependence, of the kind found in a healthy relationship to each other and to God.
4 This short poem is called 'A March Farewell', and was originally written privately in 2023 for someone who had suffered a significant loss. It is offered in a larger sense here, but with that person still very much in mind.

received in life. On the contrary, it is about seeing the precious in the sometimes paltry.

Nor is it about resenting those limits that come with our humanity and our environment – something that loss and grieving constantly reminds us of. It is about putting all of this in a new perspective. Having our imaginations and endeavours, small or large, transfigured by the untold possibilities of love.

Can Art Save the World?

So what if now, for the time being, we concluded with the not untaxing question, "How can it become possible for us wealthier human beings to deconstruct an economy of greed and live joyfully, according to the means our planet affords?"

Picking up the earlier themes of this essay, the answer has to involve systemic change, but change motivated by seeing and acting towards the whole of life as gift not possession. (It will also take will, organisation, struggle, momentum and the power of love overcoming the love of power – but that is a wider topic for now.)

In other words, paradoxically, we will likely only ever learn to live *within* our means environmentally and economically – the two are inseparable – when we learn to live hopefully and inspirationally *beyond* our means existentially. To be prepared to let go, let be and let become, both personally and collectively.

This is profoundly difficult for people reared within a technological society where there is a fix or a pill for all problems. But we are gradually beginning to realise, many of us, that the fixes and pills are not enough. Some of them may even be placebos.

In place of a conclusion (as a way-marker, therefore), confronting the truth that our lives are ones of inevitable dependence, and also that some of the problems we face will probably always be beyond us, can be very tough. Life is difficult. But it is also abundant, colourful, joyful, musical, poetic, unexpected and extraordinary. So maybe it is an immeasurable strengthening of and investment in the awareness of life's wonder which can best help us to reframe, cope and work with the unavoidable realities of difficulty, decay and death.

Living beyond our moments (realising we are not isolated), living beyond our masks (realising we do not always have to pretend) and living beyond our means (realising we are not merely the sum of our own biology and conditioning). Are these not key components of the way, the life and the truth we need most right now? If so, and for an artist of any kind, this surely means, as Michael Tippett avers, "creating images from the depths of the imagination and giving them form."

For it is only through images that the inner world communicates at all. Images of the past, shapes of the future. Images of vigour for a decadent period, images of calm for one too violent. Images of reconciliation for worlds torn by division. And in an age of mediocrity and shattered dreams, images of abounding, generous, exuberant beauty.[5]

---

5 Quoted from an essay by the composer in Oliver Soden, *Michael Tippett: The Biography* (Weidenfeld & Nicolson, 2019).

XXV
WAKEFUL POETRY

Poetry is
language
overcoming
itself. Tearing the veil
in (excess of) two.
Word-weaves touching
restless tides
beneath the torrent
of our discourse,
interrupted.
Raiding
the virtues of hesitation.
Awake of metaphor,
an eruption in defiance
of representation.
(Here is the humbling
of writing beneath
speech, dreaming
its unfathomable
plenitude...)

———

For Tina Beattie and all the poetry sisters

> *I needed my mistakes in their order to get me here.*
> – William Stanley Merwin

The mystery and possibility of poetry is unending, and for me can only be properly explained through the poetic itself, allowing space for its many spells to unfold. If this sounds dangerously close to the tautological mistake of using a term as part of its own definition, I will attempt to justify myself by revealing that the initial inspiration for this verse and its framing was actually a piece of music; one known to listeners of BBC Radio 3 as the theme tune for 'Private Passions', where guests talk about the intersection of their lives with a variety of musical experiences, and play a selection of their chosen pieces.

Unlike 'Desert Island Discs' these days (still broadcast as a staple of Radio 4), it is the music as much as the person's life story that tends to take centre stage in 'Private Passions'. Or at least, it plays a significant role in orienting the conversation and revealing how art shapes and accompanies the twists and turns of our human sojourning. Connections with literature also frequently make an appearance. So it is entirely appropriate that it is a work by presenter and composer Michael Berkeley which signals the programme's arrival on the airwaves. This is 'The Wakeful Poet' (from *Music from Chaucer*), performed by the Beaux-Arts Brass Quintet. It can also be heard performed by Onyx Brass on *Pavans, Fantasias, Variations* (Meridian Records, 2002).

For me, poetry is precisely about wakefulness, paying attention, being jolted in the direction of surprising and fresh perceptions. That includes re-readings of the everyday and matters in plain sight as much as the arc of experience or the scope of becoming and being what we are, where we are, as part of a whole tradition of linguistic exploration. In that respect, Chaucer is both of another place and time and unexpectedly of the moment. This is poetry at its time-warping best, carrying word-fabrics from the past into a reconsidered present and an as-yet-unrealised future. It is a continual invitation, in the presence of our storied lives, to wake up and dream.

To do its work, poetry not infrequently requires the disruption of an expected continuity within speech. As this particular verse emerged in my mind, I started to dipping into Jacques Derrida's infuriating *Of Grammatogy* (particularly page 71), and simultaneously found myself recalling the half-forgotten title of a short, curious comedy film made by Glenn Gould, Jock Carroll and Anatole Green in 1956, *The Virtues of Hesitation*.

But it is not all about traces, interruptions and hesitations. A poem is also a series of connections achieved by what Tina Beattie wonderfully calls "wordweaves", writing in a piece on 'Consolation and Melancholy' which landed in my inbox on 6 April 2024. That is true even when, as is the case here, the stream of thought is about the torrents of language itself, and the divisions of perception signified by the adapted biblical metaphor of "tearing the veil in (excess of) two".

The form of this verse may appear rather random, but it has elements of precision. There are exactly 50 words. These are shaped into four stanzas of five lines, running as a continuous sequence of 20 in total. Each line contains either one, two, three or four words. First came the idea. Then the rules and the language, playing off each other. The end result, I hope, is a poetic surface which operates against as well with itself in doing its work. Which must by necessity be an unfinished kind of completion.

XXVI
CHILDLESS

My children
are words set free
in the middle of the night
or early at dawn

My children
are moments wasted
with precious strangers
and curious friends

My children
are myriad notes
scored, played and sampled
among the muses

My children
are hopeful footprints
etched into the landscape
tender as snow

My children
are dreams unleashed
and loves lost or found
searching for home

My children
are tokens of love
scuttling across our lives
as the curtain fades

———

For Carla J. Roth and the Tchilingirians

Children of the world, they laugh and smile, they go to sleep with music – Yusuf Islam

Children are the emergent and evolving edge of our past, our present and our future. Without them, we would have none of those three. So there is a sense of poignancy to being, personally, childless. Yet that is what I am. An only child myself, too, the end point of a little branch of a larger family which has long dispersed itself into the winds of time past.

In my case, the decision not to have children was conscious, and shared by my beloved. The reasons are many, varied and complicated. I confess that I have rarely experienced a direct and felt connection with kids *per se*, though godson Oshin is an immeasurable gift. So I am not *quite* childless. None of us is, when we think of the family beyond family.

Nonetheless, I have no offspring. Why? In part, perhaps, because my own experience of being parented was… complicated. I was undeniably loved and wanted. But my parents had experienced many travails and traumas over the years. I have spent a lifetime negotiating what that means. It was not their fault.

Philip Larkin's 'This Be the Verse' is, of course, both right and wrong, as well as darkly funny and searingly desperate. Your mum and dad alone do not fuck you up. You are not, unless you are downtrodden in myriad other ways (which was not my experience) left with no choice but to be a victim of conditioning and genetics, nurture and Nietzsche. At least, I wasn't. But I was indeed left with scars as well as freedoms, divorce, years of rethinking and recovery, the need for injections of therapy, and then the decision itself. Me, a parent? It did not feel right. But there is a cost. An immense cost.

Some years ago, I was part of an event where someone described those of us who choose to be childless as 'selfish'. Despite its crass simplification and insulting insensitivity (from a then bishop, too), I would not deny the element of truth in that bald verdict.

XXVI CHILDLESS

For me, at least. To others, I cast no stones. We know little or nothing about the pain and struggle of others.

Yes, children are our inheritance and our destiny. They are our present, too. The demand they make is huge and the gifts they offer are (for many) immense. But they are not all there is to procreativity. That is what this poem is about. I am childless, but I still have children. Just not biological ones.

Originally, there were five verses to 'Childless'. Then I added a sixth to the five questioning orphans some months later. I cannot now remember which one, or why. It would likely have been a spark flying from a conversation, or a private thought, or a sudden realisation. There could be many more verses added, undoubtedly. You may have your own. Childless, I find that my children are, in fact, legion. This is dedicated to all those who labour outwith birthing, as well as to Oshin and his wonderful mother and father. I cannot begin to say how much I admire all parents, because I am not one.

One last thought, for the time being (which is all it ever is). Children, and their absence, are our fractured reality and our haunted dreams. As Yusuf Islam continues, in the wake of the endless, bloody, senseless parade that is the destruction of families and precious lives in Gaza and beyond: "Children wake with music. We sleep with shooting, and we wake with shooting. Despite them we will play, despite them we will play, despite them we will laugh, despite them we will sing songs of love."

XXVII

BLUE RUNES

Paint the town the aura of the sea
a slash of waveless cerulean
   mirrored to a cloudless sky
drowning, waving
   like the child with aquamarine eyes,
     lost in azure, bowing down
stardrop arms, quilted by the moon,
   seizing a calm or cruel ocean
using all the tricks the body knows
blue living on the tender earth
indigo sightings
   redrawn, day-on-day
     until we shed our wings
        cobalt parted.

For James Donald, Maria Vigers, and all my artistic and poetic friends

Beyond Our Means

> *Artists are the antennae of the human race. They sense things that are in the ether.* – Ezra Pound

I sometimes describe blue as my 'colour of significance.' In its infinite varieties, hues and textures it nearly always leaves an impression on me. When I am paying attention, at least. Blue, for me, *is* the signal to attend. It has become connected in my life and my mind to arresting, important and reframing occasions. We live between the blue of the seas and the blue of the sky, retina-framed. There is drama there. Yet what is there is also cool, and often understated. For me, blue in essence remains the colour of a paradise which is about openings rather than endings.

When I was a child, 'blue' was also my instinctive answer to the (in truth, rather meaningless) question, "what is you favourite colour?" As if we could abstract something from the rainbow and make sense of it alone. My father's choice was red, especially deep red. Politically (on this side of the Atlantic, at least) I have definitely headed in the direction of red. My current sitting room is the regal maroon that my late father loved most. It has come to mean a good deal to me in the nearly thirty years since his departure. Yet still it is blue which feels to be my home colour. When someone else gravitates 'bluewards', I usually know that we will find a connection – often one that surprises both of us, that takes some (good) work.

This poem is surreal and impressionistic. It is an attitude rather than a description, a feeling rather than a portrayal. The inclusion and attribution of different kinds of blueness is both deliberate and incidental in the way that it composed itself, though that cobalt conclusion felt inevitable. For me this 14-line verse is full of joy and foreboding, immediacy and longing, in equal measure. As I read and re-read it, new possibilities and new questions arise. Who is "the child with aquamarine eyes"? Mine are greyish. What "tricks" does the body know, and how do they work for us? This is where the runes come in. Signs, signals and portents of something mysterious at play.

XXVII BLUE RUNES

There is a definite connection between this poem and the New Apocalyptics group of poets who emerged across Britain in the 1940s, though I only really understood this when the stream of consciousness that generated it felt complete. Their style, at first dense and then simpler, reinstated myth, expressionism and surrealism in the face of dour 1930s realism. The Scottish connection included Norman MacCaig, who subsequently made what he called "a long haul back to lucidity" in his *Riding Lights* (1955).

The double dedication of 'Blue Runes' is to one person I know personally, and another I meet usually once a year. They both have studios at Coburg House in Edinburgh. James, principally a weaver by profession, provided a wonderful cover for a book I co-edited and partly co-wrote in 2020, *Scotland After the Virus*. The story of his 'mood boards', how they came about through a dog-walking photography exercise during the Covid lockdown, and how they raised money for NHS charities, is told at the beginning of that volume.[1]

Maria, on the other hand, is a talented multi-media artist who works particularly with blue. Or at least, it is her cyanotypes that always draw my attention. You can visit her creations online, as well as at shows and exhibitions. She reminds me of another person important to me who goes by that name professionally, and who was in my mind as I flurryingly penned this verse. Both James and Maria's websites are listed at the end of the book, for those who are interested. I hope you will be.

A final comment. Of all the poems in this book, this is perhaps my personal favourite: the one that says most to and about me, in my own experience and estimation. Yet I doubt that it will travel very far with others. Maybe I will be wrong about that. And what do I know anyway? It does not seem to matter. May the blue be with you.

---

1 Gerry Hassan & Simon Barrow, *Scotland After the Virus* (Luath Press, 2020). This volume includes specially commissioned poems and short stories, as well as social and political commentary.

XXVIII

LIGHTSHADOWS

Hope has many names.
A song without words
    in the land of the unresolved.
An immensity of liquid light.
The night sky's womb
    holding you close.
Skin falling upon skin,
    enfolded but unrequiting.

A question slowly rises
    as the world leans silently on your body.
More a sigh than a breath
Protesting against the dark
Tenderly breaking bread with the dead
Unravelling layers of fear
    in the cracks that reveal
        a liminal sunrise.

———

For Alice and Willard Roth, Jep and Joyce Hostetler, and their extended families

We are set in a world of loss and fire. – Flannery O'Connor[1]

The Italian philosopher Antonio Gramsci, facing down the intransigence of injustice from a prison cell, commended an attitude of tempered, positive realism that he once famously summarised as "pessimism of the intellect and optimism of the will". As Terry Eagleton points out,[2] the trajectory here is what would be better called "hope".

Hope is to be distinguished from both optimism and pessimism. Optimism in the predisposition to believe that things will work out well. Pessimism is the fear that they will turn out badly. By contrast, hope is an active investment in living well that seeks the good, the true, the beautiful, the just and the loving (interpersonally and corporately), but does not suppose that any of it will arrive gift-wrapped.[3]

In a certain sense hope is indubitably tragic, while at the very same time it is a continual protest against existential despair, political complacency and metaphysical miserabilism in the name of a better today and tomorrow. It is a practice, not a wish. It arises from a praxis that requires us to be the change we seek, and to believe not that it is inevitable (or even likely), but possible. It acknowledges the realities of failure and defeat, while refusing to capitulate to them.

A world of loss and fire is one that cuts to the heart and sears our bones. Hope is embodied, or it is nothing. This poem ultimately derives from the senses, not from speculative reason. If we are to act hopefully on any kind of sustainable basis, it will be because it has become the muscle and tissue that animates us, the taste we savour, the air we breathe, the water we swim in, the wellspring of constantly renewed imagination.

---

1 Flannery O'Connor, *The Violent Bear It Away* (Faber & Faber, 1960).
2 Terry Eagleton, *Hope Without Optimism* (Yale University Press, 2019).
3 This paragraph is adapted from an essay I published jointly with Fiona Brocklesby, 'Beyond Belief? Re-grounding a Public Politics of Hope', in (eds.) Gerry Hassan & Simon Barrow, *Britain Needs Change* (Biteback, 2024).

XXVIII   LIGHTSHADOWS

Hope is not something we pull from the sky, though it is there too. It also comes to us from tradition, and from what, within Christianity, we call "the communion of saints". Line five in the final verse of 'Lightshadows' gestures towards this truth, in an adaptation from W. H. Auden (via Seamus Heaney, Alan Jacobs and others).

As Auden says, "One of the greatest blessings conferred on our lives by the Arts is that they are our chief means of breaking bread with the dead, and I think that, without communication with the dead, a fully human life is not possible."[4]

---

[4] W. H. Auden, 'Some Reflections on the Arts' in *Prose, Volume Six, 1969–1973* (Princeton University Press, 1988).

XXIX
DEEP TIME

a volcanic catastrophe
   a disaster
      frozen in time
brooding chord clusters
    basin and range
orchestral unconformity
ages in chaos
   scales in practice
the present buried in the past
heterophonic lines intuit
   annals of the former world
reverberating in hollow snaps
hocketing textures overlap
  with erosion
     sedimentation
        formation
tempo fixed and free
  geologic violence
     blue landscape strata
no vestige of a beginning
  no prospect of an end
time's arrow
      time's circle

For Stephen Plaice and Marcia Bellamy
(and in memory of Harrison Birtwistle)

It is the stillness of an implacable force brooding over an inscrutable intention. – Joseph Conrad, Heart of Darkness

The fundamental reality and puzzle of music is that it exists inescapably in time. How time is negotiated in the changing contexts of sound defines what kind of music we are encountering, and indeed how we might need to approach it. The composer Harrison Birtwistle (1934–2022), who I miss greatly – but who left us a significant, daunting sonic legacy – often described himself as working more in cycles than with linear time.

He frequently operated with blocks of music (often cube-like) that connect or disconnect in a variety of ways, but mostly without bridging. That is true of the piece that is the direct concern of this poem, alongside the immense variety of texture, colour, rhythm and dynamics across his compositional output as a whole. Birtwistle's is an abstract, original, evolving, submerging and re-emerging musical language, at once unsettling and ear-opening.

Time itself is the subject of three of his substantial instrumental pieces, starting with *The Triumph of Time* (1972), which established him as a major compositional voice, and then the shattering *Earth Dances* (1986) fourteen years later, which I was fortunate enough to hear at its premiere, given by the BBC Symphony Orchestra at the Proms.

The last of these three pieces, *Deep Time*, followed in 2016, and is the one I chose as the subject of this verse. It is based on the notion of geologic time first proposed by the eighteenth-century Scottish geologist, James Hutton (1726–1797). Time as a geologic reality, Hutton suggested, develops as a perpetual cycle of rock erosion, sedimentation and formation. There are also catastrophes, specifically volcanic eruptions, which result in a kind of organised chaos or 'frozen violence'. I find this interesting philosophically (maybe even theologically) as well as scientifically. It also connects with the current age of meta- or poly-crisis – environmental, economic, political, psychological and spiritual.

XXIX   DEEP TIME

It is necessary to stress in this context that for Birtwistle catastrophe is not doom. So although you could say that his musical procedure is broadly modal rather than tonal, the opening of *Deep Time* is full of melodic hints and exuberance, before the darker, denser, crushing layers appear. Even then, shards of near or actual sweetness – broken up by coruscating rhythms alongside colliding swells and diminutions – keep (re)appearing as the orchestral and harmonic intensity increases. Love is omnipresent in the darkness.

Similarly, what we see as we observe the physical landscape around us is an outer beauty and "there-ness" – parallel to our own conscious "is-ness" – composed, at a deeper, structural level, out of seeming chaos, disorder, disaster and disaggregation, all "frozen in time" (line three). Yet when we dig, there is gem-like beauty, too ("blue landscape strata"). "Mountains do not rise without earthquakes", notes writer Katherine MacKennett.

While the music of *Deep Time* is not in any way programmatic or descriptive in itself, the task the composer set himself was responding musically to layers and occasions of geologic discontinuity, and the idea of there being no beginning and no end to this process (no resolution), which is how Hutton proposed it. In this regard, the penultimate couplet within the poem is taken directly from Hutton's words, followed by a slight adaptation of the title of palaeontologist Stephen Jay Gould's famous 1987 work on myth and metaphor in the discovery of geological time.

Time's Arrow is also the title of Martin Amis's 1991 life of a German Holocaust doctor presented in reverse chronology, and 'Circles of Time' is, in contrary style, from the resonant ballad by vocalist Jon Davison on the Yes album *Mirror to the Sky* (2023). There is also an accidental Star Trek reference buried in here, I have since discovered, for those who might need such a thing (though I do not). Sometimes – perhaps often – poetry stumbles upon connections it neither anticipated nor asked for.

Just as Birtwistle's music is not intended as a representation of Hutton's thesis, so my poem should not be approached as a representation of the orchestral work. The media involved do not work that way, and do not need to. They have their own voices, possibilities, procedures and (dis)continuities. But as well as taking fragments and ideas from the composer's own notes about *Deep Time* (available from his publisher, Boosey and Hawkes), I have deliberately avoided bridging lines, and I have broken up the geologic metaphors and images with musical references and inferences. It is also intentional that the poem comprises exactly 23 lines, one for each minute of the orchestral score as it is notated.

It is possible to read this poem, abstract and free as it is (or at least, as it appears to be) from end to beginning as well as from beginning to end, without a break, by reversing and continuing straight from the last line. (Then there is the notion of simply keep going and stopping in a place that is clearly not an ending, to be true to Hutton.)

In public recitation I am more than tempted to do that reversal sometimes. But in written form it feels too artificially mirrored and obvious. For the hearer the sense of a non-ending (or of revisiting the beginning, and discovering it afresh for the first time, as T. S. Eliot would put it) is emergent.

The verse naturally bends back upon itself. Or at least, that is the intention. But it does not resolve. (Birtwistle felt that non-resolution, a key aspect of geologic time, was necessarily part of his musical procedure. It is what kept him up at night, he told fellow composer Julian Anderson in a 2019 public conversation. But "I can't say it interests me in that sense, because I really like sleeping!")

This is one of two poems in this collection dealing intentionally with the evocative and delightfully disruptive music of Harrison Birtwistle. Celebrations of the 90th anniversary of his birth took place in 2024. As his publishers crisply summarised: "His sound world runs the full gamut from large-scale operatic and orches-

XXIX DEEP TIME

tral canvases, rich in mythical and primitivist power, to intimate chamber works, contemplative in their lyricism. Central artistic themes spring from his observations of cyclical forms in nature, the imaginary inner landscape, and the viewing of an object from multiple perspectives."

XXX
YEARNINGS

From every nation
From earth's wide bounds
From ocean's furthest shore
Hear what the Breath is saying

Recognise your part in the world's pain
and come home to yourselves and others
Let all that is unfree in you be released and
blossom into a future graced by love

Know your yearnings understood
For you will hunger no more
and thirst no more
in life shared

———

For everyone at St James

> *And there was a great multitude that no one could count…*
> – John the Seer

I confess that I do not warm readily to the explicit 'religious poem', though many great ones have been written. The problem for me is that what should most fully unite us (celebrating and seeking to live within the ultimacy and efficacy of love) so easily assumes forms of devotion, dogma and affiliation that lack humility and circumspection, and therefore divide and tribalise instead.

So while we must surely speak from the depths of our longings (whether we deem them 'religious' or otherwise), at the same time we should always and equally aspire to communicability, translatability, hospitality, dialogue and invitation. Many languages and dialects producing an unfathomable connectivity of difference, and therefore a larger community. Pentecost (the language of translatability) rather than Babel (the language of technocratic hierarchy), you might say.

Some of these lines are borrowed (in modified form) from ones used in the liturgy, hymnody and lectionary texts from a specific Eucharist at my local Episcopal church, St James the Less, in Leith, on Sunday 5th November 2023. Something about that service moved me to respond in this way. The poetic discipline here (because poetry is always about distilling and reordering language, even as it seeks to unleash it) is that the three verses deliberately work with increasing and then decreasing line lengths.

So these 12 lines comprise both two arrangements of six and three verses of four simultaneously. Earlier in its composition there were simply two six-line verses, but in the end, I decided it worked better the way it now is, because the first verse is essentially about widening (universality), the second is about reconciling (repairing), and the third is about realising (community). The final chosen form fitted that pattern best, with the parallel expansion and contraction somewhat mirroring the movements of scattering and gathering that inhabit many of the agricultural metaphors deployed in the gospels. (For more in this vein, see Alan Ecclestone's

XXX YEARNINGS

marvellous collection *Gather the Fragments: A Book of Days*, edited by Jim Cotter and issued by Cairns Publications in 1993.)

At the forefront of my mind as I composed this piece was the thought that there is no sustainable way of moving from the universal to the particular, or vice versa, without concrete processes of revisioning and repair: being reconciled to ourselves as to other selves. 'Hear what the breath is saying' is pivotal to such processes. That is, the breath of life itself (closer to us than that which animates our own bodies) and the larger Breath in which lies our origin, our habitation and our destiny (to slightly re-render Acts 17:28).

So 'Yearnings' is, in reality, a prayer of sorts – and one with deep roots in my own Christianly-shaped way of seeing. But equally it expresses human and universal longings which I hope that those of other faith or none (people simply of 'good faith', as a former colleague from Southwark Diocese once aptly put it) might echo with.

In terms of the borrowings: lines two and three are from verse four of the hymn 'For All the Saints' (Bishop William Walsham How, 1864); lines one, four, and nine to eleven are adapted from Revelation 7: 9–17; and the entire second verse utilises a liturgical moment from John O'Donohue, whom I acknowledge with grateful thanks. These are also words of confession and absolution employed by the good folk at St James, to whom I express enormous gratitude for embodying so much of what this says and aspires to.

XXXI
UNWOUNDING

Agnus Dei, qui tollis peccata mundi, dona nobis pacem

Imagine what would become possible
if we could but gaze on the wounds
of the other, and recognise in
them our fellow fractured
lives and likenesses?

Imagine what would become possible
if we could but see our petrified
enemies as lost and longing
kindred souls on a painful
path to siblinghood?

Imagine what would become possible
If we could but turn ourselves aside
from the vast and veiling
illusion that vengeance
ever rights wrong?

For Alison Phipps, Harry Hagopian, Clare Roberts, Siân Harris, Iain Lothian and the Pesky Piskies

Beyond Our Means

> *A great human sob shrieked in the wind, and tossed its tears upon the sea...* – W. E. B. Dubois

All the poems in this book have been written at a time when the most unspeakable horrors have been unfolding in Europe (the brutal Russian invasion of Ukraine) and the Middle East (mass slaughter in Gaza and Lebanon, with worse threatened for and with Iran). There is something surreal about watching the world around us carry on as if everything is somehow perfectly normal, while the indiscriminate killing of civilians, the targeted assassinations of health workers and journalists, large-scale collective punishment, the demolition of educational and cultural institutions, and the deliberate displacement of millions of people continues with apparent impunity. As Walter Benjamin says, "That things 'just go on' is the catastrophe."

Yes, what Hamas did on 7 October 2023 was unspeakable. But what it has been used to ignore (a whole history of occupation and oppression) and justify (limitless, unending killing and barbarity) can never be justified – and certainly not by abusing the memory of the Holocaust.[1]

As I observed in my introduction to this collection, words fail at such a moment. But the ones which fail best are usually found in verse. Or, dare I say, in prayer – by which I do not mean vain pleas to a meddling, demi-urge styled deity to sort everything out, but deep longing and searching for that sense of perspective, humanity, compassion and understanding which might enable us to address the violent dysfunctions of a politics deformed by fear and hatred.

This was expressed with disarming clarity some years ago by Abuna Elias Chacour, an Arab-Israeli who served as the Archbishop of Akko, Haifa, Nazareth and All Galilee for the Melkite Greek Catholic Church from 2006 to 2014.[2] The tragedy of the long-run-

---

[1] Naomi Klein, 'How Israel has made trauma a weapon of war', *The Guardian*, Saturday 5 October 2024.
[2] John Feister, 'Prophet of Peace: Elias Chacour' [interview], *Franciscan Media*,

XXXI UNWOUNDING

ning conflict in and around Israel-Palestine, he once said, is that the main protagonists – Palestinian Arabs and Israeli Jews – are both deeply scarred peoples whose wounds have been deepened over many generations. And yes, those wounds relate to both historical wrongs and a seemingly endless cycle of violence which requires (nay, demands) a political solution that offers dignity, freedom and justice to all.

But it is a profound failure of empathy and imagination not to realise that the repeated inability to achieve the settlement needed – either a Palestinian state alongside Israel, or a single, plural state for all – is rooted in human suffering and antagonism which, unaddressed, reinforces the heavily-armed hands of those on both sides – but specifically the colonising power – who seem relentlessly to be pursuing the path of eliminating 'the other', and therefore (it is falsely and catastrophically assumed) 'the problem'. Genocide is the ultimately uncomfortable but descriptively correct word for this.

How can just resolution and healing become possible in the face of this seemingly intractable conflict? Elias Chacour's answer is that it will only happen when, instead of seeing 'the other' as an enemy and a threat to be imprisoned or annihilated, Israelis and Palestinians alike can look into one another's eyes and recognise their own wounds in the woundedness of the other. Recognise, in other words, that beyond enmity and hate, there is a deeper brotherhood and sisterhood in suffering which, if more fully acknowledged, might free us to recognise that our own healing, security, justice, peace and safety depends precisely upon the security, justice, peace and safety of those we are continually being urged to kill, suppress or remove.

For Chacour, as a Christian, the image that comes to mind is that of enemies kneeling down together before the woundedness of the crucified Christ, and seeing at last, in a moment that can only be called revelation, that *all* wounds (ours, 'theirs' and Christ's) are

---

March 2024. https://www.franciscanmedia.org/st-anthony-messenger/prophet-of-peace-elias-chacour/

the *same* wound, and can only be repaired together. By contrast, as Martin Luther King Jr. observed, "an eye for an eye and a tooth for a tooth ends up with everyone being eyeless and toothless."

It is possible, I believe, to perceive the profound and unassailable truth of this without being the least bit naïve or wishful about the harsh realities of politics and the stubborn difficulty of achieving anything like justice for all. But ultimately the transformation of society and the transformation of the human heart cannot be separated, in Palestine-Israel or anywhere else.[3] That is what my poem 'Unwounding' is about. For as Mahmoud Darwish says, "We suffer from an incurable malady: hope."

---

3   See also: Harry Hagopian, *Keeping Faith With Hope: The Challenge of Israel–Palestine* (Ekklesia Publishing, 2019), to which I was honoured to write a publisher's foreword.

XXXII

ANTE-SUPPER

Semper dolens

Watery champagne sunlight
   peering through the sky
an angel chorus blanket
   framed by cadenced branches
trees lamenting russet and gold
the livid sheltering sky,
   dreich masquerading blue.
   (so much revealed by so little)

Darkness crawls towards afternoon
with the bunting stretching
   across South Leith Parish graves
a stone cantata on wheels
leaves settled and sodden
disciples, two by two,
   flailing before the Judas riddle
     and a strickened pink amen.

This twig accordion
   dissolves the devil's salted sermon
     into mayhem. A still
   returning Voice whispers
     theatre, ritual and psalms.
the ghost, she is us
   with our melancholy questions
   while the cold dusk cries 'Spring!'

   Semper in spe

For Robbie Mochrie and Mary Miller

> *Beauty transcends aesthetics, and is what
> inspires the best in us* – Elena Krzywon

'Ante-Supper' is another one of those poems where at least two (in this case, three) streams of consciousness flow, merge, separate and work together. It can be so confusing, yet also oddly energising, to experience such an in-spilling in one short sequence of time. And that is just for me, dear reader. Heaven knows where it leaves you. In a way, the perspective is clear. *Semper dolens, semper in spe* – always in pain, always in hope.

The respective streams in poetic play are an Autumn walk in the park, a graveyard a short distance from where I live, and the memory of Harrison Birtwistle's remarkable chamber opera, *The Last Supper*. We begin with tension between the colourful but quiet beauty of a late afternoon sun; the looming, dark-damp evening, and everything wrapped ambiguously in between.

In the second scene, and verse, we move to South Leith Parish Church (now South and North Leith, for the purists). Here there are echoes of The Smiths and the melancholic but oddly celebratory 'Cemetery Gates', where "Keats and Yeats are on your side… but you lose, 'cos wild lover Wilde is on mine." Then there are those disciples emerging curiously between the tombstones.

That is the appearance of Birtwistle. I saw a production of *The Last Supper*, with its libretto by Robin Blaser in English and Latin, at Glyndebourne 25 years ago. It was the only time I got to talk to the composer, briefly, afterwards. So it is etched in my mind. The drama is a kind of 're-union' retelling of the biblical story, but with an open textured narrative that rests on the unresolved.

An ethereal ghost character, who represents all of us in a way, invites the disciples to another supper, two by two. Uncertainty ensues. Whence this invitation? Will Judas be there… will Christ be there? How on earth will that go? What will happen this time? The dramatic tension lies in juxtaposing the old and the new, the Jewish and Christian, and what has occurred in the elapsing of two thousand years of history since the original meal took place. The story of Christianity is tortuous and blemished. Blood has been shed. Bread has not been shared.

Birtwistle's operatic recreation, poised irresolvably between belief and scepticism, ends in the Garden of Olives. Christ asks, "Whom do you seek?" Then a cock crows. The betrayal, it seems, continues. In my mind's eye, and in the poem, the story unfolds for a third time between the Autumn leaves, in the gusting wind, through the graveyard and into a new promise of Spring. The invitation to the Feast. Again. Before and after…

XXXIII

PIERCED BEAUTY

Being present
   has re-opened
      my imagination
To an urban sunrise
To the music of trees
To moments full of flowers
To the whisper of a blue moon
To the shadowlands of our secret self
To passion and yearning and unquenchable thirst
To desire within desire and a thorn lacerating the heart.
To poetry
   after pain
      (and before pity).

For Carla J. Roth

*We have to try to cure our faults by attention
and not by will.* – Simone Weil

Before we married thirty years ago, Carla presciently gave me a copy of Jon Kabat-Zinn's book, *Wherever You Go, There You Are* (Hachette, 1994). She noticed something I lacked, and probably still do. It would be fair to say that I never read the book, but unfair to say that it – or at least it's title – has not had an impact on me, most especially through the more philosophically attuned adjacent writings of Simone Weil. For her, attention is perhaps the greatest gift and necessity in discovering what it is to live a good life.

By contrast, too much of my 67 years on this planet so far have consisted of distraction punctuated by episodes of concentration, rather than the other way around. This is not without its gains. Attention can be scattered as well as condensed. The butterfly mind can collect many gifts and make myriad connections. But without the ability to focus on bringing all this together, and supplementing it through the deep-dive of disciplined living and study, so much will be missed or misconstrued. The same principle applies to one's immediate environment and the curation of the present moment.

Gradually, I have learned this. Being where I am. Poetry can achieve that. So can photography. Carla still feels that when I suddenly whip out my cameraphone on a walk (which is often) I am being distracted again. This is true, in part. But it is also a result of noticing, and wishing to be able to benefit as fully as possible from the impact of what has drawn my attention, to be saturated by an encounter with the vivid present.

A not dissimilar process happens with music, though it can be a struggle these days. When I was growing up, there was a ritual to acquiring a new album. First, the search. Talking and investigating with others, a visit to the record shop, the selection of a piece of music, and then the commitment to what the music demanded through listening completely and fully. In my teenage and later

XXXIII PIERCED BEAUTY

years this would often happen in the evening, by candlelight. The first side, then the second, then repeat… until the notes, chords, harmonies, clusters, melodies, rhythms, dissonances and contrapuntal layers somehow entered my being. Some of them became part of me, and stayed for a lifetime.

These days, digital and streaming media mean that virtually any piece of music you may wish to consider is available almost instantly (and often with far too little financial reward to its composer or creators). The personal problem here is the capacity and temptation to skim, skip and scrape. This is not listening. It is not attention. It is not being encountered and changed. It is not fully being where you are.

This particular poem has a directness which I do not find entirely comfortable. Pierced indeed, and maybe not with as much beauty as I crave. I would probably prefer to hide behind 'better' words. But these were the ones that came to me in the moment. I have decided to let them be. Wherever they go, there I am.

XXXIV

AUTUMNISING

As summer recedes, last-lighted,
    the neighbourhood turns
        orange, brown, yellow and purple.
A red nasturtium leaf nestles defiantly
    in the sprawling dank.
Broken sunflower leaves curl
    away from hurrying, passing feet,
        refusing a bleak afternoon.
Mist, rain, stormclouds and chill winds beckon.
Twirls of sunlight peering between
    swollen twigs and branches
Trees shivered to a bare-stripped spine
Seasoning the will to approaching frost
Attuning us to shadowglow
    and *O Magnum Mysterium*.

For the wound and the gift again,
from a coffee shop in Lewes

In Heaven, it is always Autumn. – John Donne

Summer is where I began. Autumn was where I thought I had got to in terms of some kind of wrap. Then Winter (the cold began to reach my bones), uncertain Spring, and another summer turned to dust. On 11 July, to be precise. In a coffee shop as I floundered for words.

So a quite different kind of Autumn came again. Not the one I wanted. One where the vivid colours turned to dust. All I can do, therefore, is to invoke the full range of russet hues once again, and ask them to re-inhabit my crumbling mind. Maybe she has gone for ever. Then again, maybe she has not. I need to remind myself that within the full, beauteous weave that Autumn reminds us of before the Winter falls, what I love more deeply than 'feelings' exists, even (perhaps especially, and in her own way) without me.

Nevertheless, I long for those "twirls of sunlight". And when I can no longer see them, when everything seems bleak, there will be, somehow, the shadowglow. I just wish you could see what I can see, and could bathe in its glorious invitation. There is so much living to do. Yes, in the twilight years. That is where seasonal in poetry rests, for me at least. I will not pretend to a great bond with nature. I am more like an urban rat, sniffing the ground. But when I look up, even I cannot miss the intimations of magic in those rich, rainbow-less colours.

If Heaven is Autumn, someone will have to show it to me, I am afraid. *O Magnum Mysterium*. My eyes are too dim right now. The cold is still deep set. But Spring will come again. Somehow. The rest is mere commentary.

The shadow and the light…

XXXV

LAKESONG

The lake is full of murmurs
Salted, soft and starting to sing
One last dream of earthy paradise
On a sunlit midday shore.
Shaped by marvelglinting crystals
In the lantern's dim diminished sight
These blossoming daiquiri waters
Are the music's mindglow.

He composes as if waiting for an infinite
Orchestrating bodies that float across the stage
Fresh formed, fluid, febrile
The rising, falling pitter-pattered rototoms
Hint sunlight out of water
Pulses for a song without words
Time past, present and future
As the lake's call echoes from the sky.

God hides, some will say
In this pink translucent light
Between the shadow and the soul
Clouds and clocks measure movement
Across the wisening sky
The water will change us if we are
Porous to its soundful silence
An earglow born of exile.

The lake is full of song
Shimmering, sighing, ecstatic
From whitish green to blushing rose
A luminous eyeglow between

Our approaching shadows
Walking to the paradise garden
A sleephaze chanson
Diminuendo, the sense of an ending…

(plop)

―――――――

For Oliver Soden and Sally Groves (in memory of Michael Tippett)

XXXV LAKESONG

Music is the most immediate expression of the noumenal self.
– Arthur Schopenhauer

Though I will likely change my mind about this the next time anyone asks, if I had only one piece of music to take with me into the rest of my days, it probably would be Michael Tippett's glorious swansong, *The Rose Lake*. This is, of course, a ridiculous conceit, in the venerable meaning of that word. But it is one we use to express to ourselves and those around us quite how deeply etched a work of art is in our soul.

The music of Michael Tippett has loomed large in my life for many decades.[1] But it is the world premiere of this marvellous "song for orchestra without words", his final major work,[2] that stands out in my emotional memory. It took place at London's Barbican Centre on Sunday 19 February 1995, with Colin Davis conducting the London Symphony Orchestra. This was the culmination of a short festival in celebration of Tippett's 90th birthday, under the title 'Visions of Paradise', drawn from Milton's explorations of the myth of the golden age.

Though I have heard many live performances of *The Rose Lake* over the past 30 years, in truth the details of the very first one have not stayed with me. But what happened right at the end is indelibly stamped upon my mind. As the very last note of the piece died away, two young fogeys in the gallery (part of a group who had been disrupting contemporary music concerts for some time) shouted out "visions of hell!" I remember the sickness in my stomach at that moment. Michael Tippett was sitting a couple of rows in front of me, to my right. As people looked at him in bemusement, he brushed aside the heckle with a light, dismissive

---
1 I hope that my long-gestated *Transfiguring the Everyday: The Musical Vision of Michael Tippett* (Siglum) will appear very soon. The Michael Tippett Musical Foundation is also most worthy of support: www.tippettfoundation.org.uk
2 'The Rose Lake' was not written as a conscious "last work". It could be argued that Michael Tippett's great, unsung (for too long) summing-up was *The Mask of Time*, a kind of metamodern post-oratorio that is very much its own musical creature. It is what looking inside the composer's head might have sounded like, I have always felt.

hand gesture, while the appreciative audience drowned out the yelling in applause.

Almost every time I recount this, I have to hold back tears. But in the end, in defiance of the hecklers' pathetic malevolence, it was a moment of triumph for Tippett and for his paradisical musical aesthetic in this remarkable 29-minute work.

The Rose Lake was inspired by the composer's visit to Lake Retba (popularly known as Le Lac Rose, or the Rose Lake) in Senegal. It is so named because, under certain conditions during the day, the salt-water lake manifests varying shades of pink, from dull to translucent. Tippett uses the orchestra, and a huge row of 38 ro-totoms tuned across five octaves, to explore a variety of captivating textures, melodies and sonorities that capture the lake at different times during the day.

He said at the time: "I was able to formulate a musical structure whose main stages I risked identifying with captions: 'The lake begins to sing', 'The lake song is echoed from the sky', 'The lake is in full song', 'The lake song leaves the sky', and 'The lake sings itself to sleep'. All this may sound naïve, but in fact the titles signify an important dimension to what might otherwise be summarised as a continuous five-part composition… in essence a set of variations. The descriptive captions finally suggested an overall subtitle for the piece: 'A song without words for orchestra'… One can [also] think of the piece as also manifesting a progression from dawn to dusk."[3]

'Lakesong' loosely follows this structure, using words and phrases more than notes and chords to work its atmosphere. There is an allusion in there to György Ligeti, who was celebrated in a Barbican season alongside Tippett back in 1995. His textural landscapes and expressionism produce a musical language very different to that of the English composer, while sharing its visionary character. I love them both. "God hides" is adapted from a piece

---

[3] Quoted by John Mangum in his programme note for the Los Angeles Philharmonic Association. https://www.laphil.com/musicdb/pieces/4179/the-rose-lake

by Robert Fripp. Meanwhile, 'sunlight out of water' references (in reverse) the title for Meirion Bowen's orchestral re-arrangement of Tippett's String Quartet No. 4. As for the final word of the poem, this is Tippett's. 'Plop' was what scribbled for the last brass note at the conclusion of his score.

I am conscious of how foolish it is to seek to wax poetic about a great work of art in another form; especially one that purposefully seeks to resonate *without* words. Whatever its deficiencies, my hope is that this will at least encourage a few more people to experience Tippett's music for themselves (best of all live) and to discover Oliver Soden's luminous biography[4] of one of the most important voices of twentieth century composition.

---

4 Oliver Soden, *Michael Tippett: The Biography* (Weidenfeld & Nicolson, 2019).

XXXVI

TRANSFIGURED

Before the dimming hour
having loved life with abandon
cherished friendship deeply
endured trials of worth
given love to those who
needed it most
left soft shoesteps
on the fragile earth
and bequeathed such lessons
as living considered with
a degree of care and honesty
can smoke-trail behind
a last breath
I will be ready
for the journey of sweet oblivion
destined by the dark passage
into a strangely
companioned light
(may I so learn)

---

*For Carla J. Roth (in memory of Ann Stricklen
and others we miss deeply)*

To pay attention, this is our endless and proper work. – Mary Oliver

What does it mean to live a good life? The answer will differ for each person. But good is certainly more than happy, content or care-free. For the great majority who have lived or will live in this world, moments of fulfilment, pleasure or joy (these three differ) may dwell for a time, but momentarily. For some they will be virtually absent. Because life is also tragic. As much a repository of bitterness and loss as sweetness and satisfaction.

No, goodness arises when we begin to think about how we might see the tragic everyday transfigured. It comes from what we have the capacity to give, not what we have the desire to take. In fact, more and more, we may discover that the taking *is* the giving. Not as in the pious sentiment that "it is better to give than to receive", but in the realisation that the distinction dissolves when we are giving and receiving the right things.

Can a gift be given? Giving and receiving have to be more than a transaction to be anything at all. This is where we touch, see, smell, hear and taste what really is "right and good". This poem is therefore about the small, insignificant footsteps which may remain, for a time at least, when we have gone – because they have, indeed, proven right and good in the lives of others. Their depth and endurance in a public sense should not matter.

If we have touched someone with care, transformed something out of love, striven to see some small justice prevail, trodden lightly on a fragile earth, borne human life with and for others in some degree, moved from measurement to metaphor in treating life well, shared some learning, or bequeathed a piece of creativity which consoles or inspires… then we have sewn the seeds of a good life which can never be ours alone, but will always be experienced – gift upon gift – in the 'together' for which we exist.

As for the moment of departure, the dark passage. That is not of our time or making. We can but wish to have grown a little more soulful when it happens, to be open to the light that continues

XXXVI TRANSFIGURED

to shine outwith and beyond us, inviting us home. The good, the true and the beautiful are our origin, our companion and our destiny. That I truly believe. Help my unbelief.

Aftersong: Poems (Mostly) Without Words

Music does certain things which even the greatest literature may not.
— George Steiner

WHAT NOTE should an afterword to a collection of poetry and prose, strike? Words have surely run their natural course. Why more? Time for sound to find its own timbres, hues and resonances. For me, the first art is silence. And out of silence, deep in the heart, there is music. At its best, like poetry, this repositions sound and silence against the encroachment of mere noise. I could not live without music, or if I could, I would not want to. Music surpasses and envelopes words, concepts, semantics and sense-making. Where lyrics and librettos exist, they are framed, elevated and carried by sonority. Music expresses feelings we never knew we had, and projects the soul beyond all worlds. It is indeed poetry in motion, and specifically vibration.

Well, not all music is like this. Some entertains, accompanies or sells, but little more. There is nothing inherently wrong in that – though the selling sometimes grates hard, and ruins any real possibility of art happening. As Glenn Gould has said: "The purpose of art is not the release of a momentary ejection of adrenaline but rather the gradual, lifelong construction of a state of wonder."[1] You do not play the piano with your fingers, but with your mind, he suggested. Maybe, in a sense, the piano, or any instrument, plays

---

[1] Glenn Gould, quoted from his typically provocative article 'Let's Ban Applause!' from *Musical America* (1962). He added "serenity" to "wonder", which is legitimate. But so would be "disturbance", in a creative sense. New ways of perceiving may be awe-inspiring, but they can be far from comfortable or serene. That said, I long ago made my peace with so-called dissonance.

you. Just as a composition or improvisation comes from you, but only after it has come to you. To those who truly listen, music finds its muses. Poetry, too.

The music that truly endures for me, that never fails to shape and inspire me, is the kind that in some sense moves heart, mind and body together. Though the classical traditions (yes, plural) are foundational for me (mostly but not exclusively in their Western forms), music that matters crosses into my life from many sources and places. Jazz, art rock, electronica, Carnatic, ambient, psychedelic, post-minimalist, experimental… and the various breeds that pass for 'new music' or 'contemporary classical' these days. Much of what connects with me personally is what might otherwise be described as "high information music". Complexity, riddles and layerings compel. But then again, a simple ballad or a perfectly crafted pop song[2] are sometimes what the soul needs, too.

Music for a Desert Island

Since fame is something I have neither sought nor acquired, my secret fantasy of appearing on BBC Radio 4's 'Desert Island Discs' or BBC Radio 3's 'Private Passions' (see xxv. 'Wakeful Poetry') will, along with many others, remain unfulfilled. But the discs that would accompany me into solitude are forever sifting and shifting in the playlist of my mind. For you too, probably. Because this selection is in my imagination, the specific rules that apply in the former programme, particularly, are able to pass me by. So in this final flourish and indulgence, I will weave a few thoughts around eight CDs, not merely tracks, which have meant (and often mended) the world to me over six decades.

The first choice has to be G. F. Handel. When I was nine or ten years old, I became obsessed with three Decca discs of the Opus 4

---

2 Robert Wyatt of rock-fusion experimentalists Soft Machine, and other musical adventures, said in the BBC documentary *Prog Britannia: An Observation in Three Movements* (2012) that people supposed – because of the kind of music he wrote and played – that he must despise pop music. On the contrary, he said, he was in awe of those who could write a perfect pop song. He was just not one of them.

and 7 organ concertos, recorded in the 1950s and early 1960s by the late, much-missed Karl Richter and his Chamber Orchestra. They were by turns grand, stately, gentle and exuberant. But my introduction to Handel had actually been his *Ode for Saint Cecilia's Day*, performed by the Academy of St Martin in the Fields under the baton of Richard Willcocks (Decca, 1968). It still spurs me forward if I am feeling low today.[3]

My parents had brought me up a on a solid diet of Bach, Mozart, Haydn, Beethoven, Brahms, Mendelssohn, Schubert and Schumann. One afternoon, venturing into a record store on a family holiday in Eastbourne, I chanced upon an LP with an abstract slash of black on the cover, cutting across an uneven golden daubing. My 13-year-old self loved its in-your-face modernism. The record was Bartok's *Violin Concerto No. 2*, played by Susanne Lautenbacher and the Radio Luxemburg Orchestra, paired with *Contrasts for Clarinet, Violin and Piano* (Turnaround, 1972). My parents told me I would hate it. I bought it anyway, took it home, put it on my turntable and was utterly bemused at first. But determined not to be proven wrong, I listened again and again until a very different kind of melodic and harmonic sound world began to impress itself upon me and win my commitment, carried forward by its propulsive and angular rhythms.

Another favourite from my teenage years which has stayed with me ever since was Ravel's *Piano Concerto in G*, together with the *Concerto for the Left Hand* (CFP, 1960), recorded by Samson François with the Paris Conservatoire Orchestra under André Cluytens. It was the G Major concerto that partly helped move me into jazz a decade later. Its lingering, achingly beautiful slow movement is as poetic as anything in the repertoire, save perhaps the opening of the Tippett Concerto for Piano and Orchestra (1955), with its otherworldly celeste.

Next on my desert island selection is something completely different. Like many youngsters of my generation I was seduced by

---

3 Maybe along with a quick dose of anarcho-punk from Chumbawamba! Sometimes, music just has to be pure adrenalin.

progressive rock, and in particular Yes in the 1970s. The four-track, 1973 Atlantic double-album *Tales From Topographic Oceans* is in my view a masterpiece of its kind. From the chant-like opening of 'The Revealing Science of God' right through the emotionally powerful denouement of 'Ritual' (taking in the respective sonar folk and Eastern-inflected dissonant sonorities of 'The Remembering' and 'The Ancient', respectively, along the way) it is one extraordinary, explorative musical journey. While the genre as a whole may have descended into bombast and absurdity at times, it also produced some absolute gems. This is one of them.

The fifth of my eight discs would have to be something from Miles Davis, perhaps the single most galvanising figure in modern jazz. Strong contenders would be the classic *Kind of Blue* album, released on 17 August 1959 through Columbia Records. This pioneered the shift towards modal jazz. But unlike some of those who appreciated the early genius of Miles, plus his evolution through fusion and experimental idioms, I do not dismiss his later work, which incorporated and transformed many varieties of popular music and made them shine in quite unexpected ways. The 1985 Warner Brothers album *Tutu*, substantially a collaboration with bassist/composer Marcus Miller, stands out here.

My specific choice would be the extended, 17-minute version of the short title track, as performed on *That's What Happened – Live In Germany* (Mercury Studios, 1987). Miles floats across the stage, conjuring magic from a highly talented band that raises this comparatively straightforward, funk-inflected music to new heights through their intense ability to listen to each other, bringing something magical yet organic in the combination and solo slots. One of my great regrets is never seeing Miles (or Frank Zappa) live. He can still be recognised from virtually a single note. The final album released in his lifetime, *Aura* (Columbia, 1989), produced by Danish composer/trumpeter Palle Mikkelborg, is noteworthy for its icy-but-colourful orchestrally textural edge.

The next choice is particularly difficult. György Ligeti's groundbreaking *Atmosphères* (1961), which employs micropolyphonic

Aftersong: Poems (Mostly) Without Words

'sound masses' in place of conventional melody, harmony and pulse. Or John Coltrane's *A Love Supreme* (1965), closely followed in my estimation by *My Favourite Things* (1961)? Or Allan Holdsworth's guitarsynth fantasy, *Secrets* (Intima Records, 1989)? Impossible though it is, I personally edge towards Holdsworth, a musician of quite exceptional facility and musicality who had me completely under his spell whenever I saw him live. He combined a harmonic language befitting a contemporary classical musician with the improvisational dexterity of a jazz musician and the drive of a rock musician. But *Secrets* is also about nuance, legato fluidity and (on the title track) the exquisite voice of Rowanne Mark. I cannot be without Allan.[4]

That brings me to the final two discs. This collection already references in some detail three works by Harrison Birtwistle which are among those most important to me. His definitive opera *The Mask of Orpheus* (xxii. 'Orpheus Untold'), searing orchestral work *Deep Time* (xxix), and chamber opera *The Last Supper* (xxxii. 'Ante-Supper'). For my desert island, I will go with a fourth angle. This is pianist Joanna MacGregor and the Radio Filharmonisch Orkest performing *Antiphonies for Piano and Orchestra* along with *Nomos* and *An Imaginary Landscape* with the BBC Symphony Orchestra, conducted by Paul Daniel (Collins Classics, 1994). More glorious puzzles from a genuine enigma of English music. Truly a lifetime's musical absorption in 68 minutes.

Last, but foremost for me, has to be Michael Tippett. The *Ritual Dances*, excerpted from his glorious first opera, *The Midsummer Marriage*, have long been an immovable fixture in my desert island selection. Their urgent lyricism, additive rhythms, contrapuntal contrasts and moments of dissolving beauty were what first drew me towards the composer's highly individual musical language, which then shifted starkly in his second opera, *King Priam*. It headed in challenging directions that "embraced modernity but reflected tradition, resisted tonality but eluded theoretical and his-

---

[4] I am honoured to have been involved in supporting the publication of Ed Chang, *Devil Take the Hindmost, The Otherworldly Music of Allan Holdsworth* (FMS Edition, 2020).

torical understandings of atonality, and, most significantly, constructed a ... remarkably broad aesthetics."[5]

Then at the end of his composing life Tippett moved back towards an almost unabashed lyricism, but in a quite transformed and transforming way, via his endlessly subtle tone poem *The Rose Lake*, "a song for orchestra without words". I have explored this piece earlier in xxxv. 'Lakesong', along with *The Blue Guitar* (ix. 'Wired'). In 2005, Chandos helpfully released a marvellous pairing of *The Rose Lake* and the *Ritual Dances*, performed by the BBC National Orchestra of Wales under the baton of Richard Hickox. This would have to be my first desert island choice, and the one that would remain with me if all others were swept away by the elements.

So those are (currently) the pieces that form my musical foundation, one could say. They sink into my bones and run along the edges of the world with me. They are all, in different ways, poetic to the core. But the transforming, juggling and dreaming never stops. Music rises and falls within our consciousness; appearing for a season, apparently disappearing, and then returning to bring something unexpectedly fresh from the familiar.

Ad Libtum

I have already indicated, *inter alia*, some of the recordings which almost made the final (cruel) cut. To those I would have to add two that were on the list earlier in life: Poulenc's most popular *Gloria* and his wonderful *Concerto for Organ, Strings and Timpani*, with Maurice Duruflé at the console (EMI, 1964), and Fauré's *Requiem*, with Victoria de los Angeles (soprano) and Dietrich Fischer-Dieskau (baritone) from CFP in 1976. As with the Ravel piano concerti mentioned above, the latter is performed by the Orchestra of the Paris Conservatoire conducted by André

---

[5] A comment from Kenneth Gloag, reviewing David Clarke, *The Music and Thought of Michael Tippett: Modern Times and Metaphysics* (Cambridge University Press, 2001), in *Music Theory Online*, Volume 10, Number 2, June 2004. https://mtosmt.org/issues/mto.04.10.2/mto.04.10.2.gloag.html

Cluytens. The organ part of the 'In Paradisum' was played, at my suggestion and request, for my mother's funeral in 1978.

Ranking close to Tippett in my affections, alongside Ligeti, are Messiaen and Takemitsu. The *Turangalîla-Symphonie* and *Le Banquet Céleste* for organ (thank you, John Garner) were among the many works of Messiaen that transported me to another world when I first heard them. For Tōru Takemitsu, it has to be *From Me Flows What You Call Time*, his 1990 concerto for five percussionists and orchestra which I experienced at the Royal Albert Hall on 15 August 1993, with the BBC Symphony Orchestra conducted by Andrew Davis, also a supreme champion of Tippett. This was recorded and issued by the BBC's *Music* magazine in 1994.

From Me Flows What You Call Time is undoubtedly music entwined with visual performance poetry. After a brief flute solo at the beginning, the percussionists enter the hall, each wearing a colour pocket square of a different hue (blue for water, red for fire, yellow for earth, green for wind, and white for sky). In the same colours are long ribbons, linking the stage to bells and chimes hung from the ceiling. Later, the ribbons are used to ring these bells. The piece ends only when the last chime to sound is still. Witnessing this was one of the most profound moments of my life. But no recording could ever capture it, which is perhaps why it has to reside in my memory first and foremost.

Of almost equal atmospheric and emotional weight is the remarkable 1993 Celestial Harmonies issue of *Sounds & Sweet Airs (That Give Delight and Hurt Not)*, recorded late at night in Southwark Cathedral on 30 and 31 May 1992. This features pieces from what was Shakespeare's parish church, then simply St Mary the Virgin, composed by Ian Carr (trumpet, flugelhorn), John Taylor (organ) and the distant thunder around them. It is also the coming together of the worlds of jazz and classical music in an entirely natural and unforced way, which is too rare. That in turn reminds me of the 2004 live album *Scorched*, artfully fusing composition and improvisation from composer Mark-Anthony Turnage and jazz guitar polymath John Scofield, with the Frankfurt Radio Symphony

Orchestra (who commissioned it in 2002), John Patitucci on bass, and Pete Erskine on drums.

Talking of percussion and drums, how can I pass on Bill Bruford, who not only created outstanding albums with Yes and King Crimson, but went on to make a pioneering contribution to jazz (or 'interactive music', as he now prefers it[6]) with the electro-acoustic and acoustic versions of Earthworks? He has also collaborated with Allan Holdsworth in the band Bruford, Patrick Moraz (*Music for Piano and Drums*, 1983), The New Percussion Group of Amsterdam (*Go Between*, 1987), Eddie Gomez and Ralph Towner (*If Summer Had Its Ghosts*, 1997), the World Drummers Ensemble (*A Coat of Many Colours*, 2006), composer Colin Riley and Piano Circus (*Skin and Wire*, 2009), and many more. This is an incredibly rich and varied tapestry of music, both as a performer and writer. Perhaps the best way to taste it is in one of his several career-curating boxed sets.[7]

Companions in the Tuned Ether

And so it continues. Thea Musgrave, Hildegard of Bingen, Patricia Alessandrini, Deirdre Cartwright, Julia Wolfe, Barbara Thompson, Freya Waley-Cohen, Carleen Anderson, Elisabeth Lutyens, Barbara Higbie, Kaija Saariaho, Ella Fitzgerald, the hugely underrated Priaulx Rainier, Joni Mitchell, Carola Bauckholt, Judith Weir, Suzanne Vega, Barbara Hannigan (in case you were rightly wondering where the women were).

Then there is Praetorius' *Terpsichore* (1612), Jason Rebello's startling debut *A Clearer View* (1990), Janacek's *Jenufa* (1902), Tangerine Dream's *Phaedra* (1973), Ornette Coleman's *Free Jazz: A Collective Improvisation* (1960), Pierre Boulez's *Pli Selon Pli* (1960 and be-

---

6 Jason Barnard, 'Bill Bruford on Reinvention and Returning to Music', *The Strange Brew*, 14 October 2024. https://thestrangebrew.co.uk/bill-bruford-on-returning-to-music/

7 Details may be found at https://billbruford.com. Also highly recommended, for those interested in exploring the psychology, practice and cultivation of creativity in music is his book *Uncharted: Creativity and the Expert Drummer* (University of Michigan Press, 2018).

Aftersong: Poems (Mostly) Without Words

yond), Steely Dan's *Aja* (1977), Godspeed You! Black Emperor's *Lift Your Skinny Fists Like Antennas to Heaven* (2000), Schoenberg's *Moses und Aron* (from 1923), Sting's extraordinary live album (with an array of jazz talent) *Bring on the Night* (1985), Varèse's *Ionisation* (1931), Billie Holiday's 'Strange Fruit' (1939), Goldie's *Timeless* (1985), Frank Zappa's Boulez collaboration, *The Perfect Stranger* (1984), Debussy's *La Mer* (1905), Porcupine Tree's *Coma Divine* (1997), George Crumb's *Black Angels* and *Ancient Voices of Children* (both 1970), Sheppard / Lodder / Vasconcelos' 'Where We Going', from *Inclassifiable* (1994), King Crimson's *THRaKaTTaK* (1996), Montreux's *Live at Montreux* (1985), Björk Guðmundsdóttir's *Homogenic* (1997), Webern's complete works (released by CBS in 1978), Ozric Tentacles' 'Throt' on *Live Underslunky* (1992) and 'Lost in in the Sky' from A38 Ship (2013),[8] Captain Beefheart's *Trout Mask Replica* (1969), Brand X's *Cambodia* (1980), Bach's *The Well-Tempered Clavier* (1772) and so much by Stravinsky.

Any of those and more, though remarkably different from one another (I have deliberately mixed them up to emphasise that) are works that nourish a portion of me, and together reach out towards the whole, without ever filling it. That is how music works for many people now. Not primarily in terms of genres or towering canons, but as part of an evolving, morphing diet that satisfies through its range, capacity and reach. There is hope for continuing enrichment here, as well as the risk of a diffusion of quality. (I am talking with and to those who love and engage with ordered sound centrally, rather than those for whom it is more ephemeral or additional).

So music is an endless journey in and of itself. But more than that, it embodies a variety of ways of travelling in the company, sympathy and surprise of others. As soon as I lay down my metaphorical pen from this Aftersong, I will think of more pieces that changed me, and regret not mentioning them. Like poetry, what endures sonically does so because it adds sinew to your life; perhaps im-

---

[8] Performed live, with the wonderful Brandi Wynne on bass, at A38 Ship, Budapest, Hungary. https://www.youtube.com/watch?v=KINkuVZ47-k

perceptibly, but nevertheless in ways which make a difference to what you yourself might be able to bequeath to others. Picking up and putting down, making impressions, leaving footprints, letting go, gathering the fragments. These are the metaphors – poetic, musical, philosophical and artistic in the broad sense – by which we might be able to make some useful contribution to the flow of living before it takes us in its arms once more and subdues us, or propels us into the Light.

Further Reading

MANY OF THE BOOKS and texts listed below, in gloriously uncommitted alphabetical order, are referenced in the 40 prose pieces contained within this collection. Others have been added from my recent reading, and from the small poetry collection I have nurtured as part of my personal library over many years. A good number are not, in themselves, poetry, but deal with language, writing, art, hope and a dozen other poetically-adjacent concerns which have informed, inspired or tempered what I have ventured in these pages. All these editions cited are the ones I have read or consulted. A number were originally penned and first published many years earlier.

>Dante Alighieri, *The Divine Comedy* (1321, Gutenberg Project 2023).
>Martin Amis, *Time's Arrow* (Vintage, 2003).
>Maya Angelou, *And Still I Rise* (Random House, 1978).
>W. H. Auden, 'Some Reflections on the Arts' in *Prose, Volume Six, 1969–1973* (Princeton University Press, 1988).
>Khawla Badwan & Alison Phipps, *Keep Telling of Gaza* (Sidhe Press, 2024).
>James Baldwin, *The Fire Next Time* (Penguin Modern Classics, 1971).
>Simon Barrow, *Against the Religion of Power: Telling a Different Christian Story* (Ekklesia Publishing, forthcoming 2025).
>_____, *Solid Mental Grace: Listening to the Music of Yes* (Cultured Llama, 2018).
>Adriana Barton, *Wired for Music* (Greystone, 2022).

Gwendolyn Bennett, *Nocturnes and Other Verse* (Forgotten Press, 2024).
Wendell Berry, *Selected Poems* (Counterpoint, 1999).
_____, *The Peace of Wild Things* (Penguin, 2018).
Betty Birch, *We Save Bits of String* (St Christopher Press, 2011).
William Blake, *Songs of Innocence and Experience* (Tate Publishing, facsimile, 2006).
J. Bronowski, *William Blake* (Penguin, 1968).
Ernesto Cardenal, *Apocalypse and Other Poems* (New Directions, 1977).
_____, *Nicaraguan New Time: Poems* (Journeyman, 1988).
Elias Chacour, *Blood Brothers* (Baker Books, 2022).
Joseph Conrad, *Heart of Darkness* (Reader's Library Classics, 2001).
Gillian Court, *Heart of Flesh* (CTBI, 2008).
e. e. cummings, *Selected Poems, 1923–1958* (Faber & Faber, 1977).
Jacques Derrida, *Of Grammatology* (Johns Hopkins University Press, 2016).
John Donne, *The Complete English Poems* (Penguin Classics, 1976).
W. E. B. Du Bois, *Black Reconstruction in America* (Free Press, 1999; first edn. 1935).
Geoffrey Duncan, *A World of Blessing* (Canterbury Press, 2000).
Terry Eagleton, *Hope Without Optimism* (Yale University Press, 2019).
_____, *How to Read a Poem* (Wiley-Blackwell, 2006).
Alan Ecclestone, *Gather the Fragments: A Book of Days* (Cairns Publications, 1993).
Louise Erdrich, *Original Fire: Selected and New Poems* (Harper, 2004).
T. S. Eliot, *Four Quartets* (Faber & Faber, 1944).
_____, *Selected Poems* (Faber & Faber, 1975).
_____, *The Waste Land* (Faber & Faber, 2022).

Further Reading

C. Litton Falkiner, *Poetry of Thomas Moore* (Macmillan, 1903).
Barry Feinberg, *Poets to the People: South African Freedom Poems* (George Allen & Unwin, 1974).
David Fideler, 'How Beauty Can Save Us' in *Living Ideas Journal* (n.d.)
Sarah Lee Brown Fleming, *Clouds and Sunshine* (US Library of Congress, 1920).
Marya E. Gates, 'Marilyn Monroe's Truth Was in Her Poetry' (*Vulture*, 12 October 2022).
W. H. Gardner (ed.). *Gerard Manley Hopkins: Selected Poems* (Penguin, 1968).
David Goldstein, *The Jewish Poets of Spain* (Penguin, 1965).
John Goodby, *The Collected Poems of Dylan Thomas: The Centenary Edition* (Weidenfeld & Nicolson, 2019).
Harry Hagopian, *Keeping Faith With Hope: The Challenge of Israel-Palestine* (Ekklesia Publishing, 2019).
Tara Hanks, 'Made in Paris': Was Marilyn a Secret Francophile? *The Marilyn Report*, 16 July 2022).
David Bentley Hart, *The Beauty of the Infinite* (Eerdmans, 2003).
_____, *Roland in Moonlight* (Angelico Press, 2021).
_____, *All Things Are Full of Gods: The Mysteries of Mind and Life* (Yale University Press, 2024).
Gerry Hassan & Simon Barrow, *Scotland After the Virus* (Luath Press, 2020).
Seamus Heaney, *Death of a Naturalist* (Faber & Faber, 1966).
Sarah Henstra, *We Contain Multitudes* (Little, Brown & Co., 2020).
Edward Hirsch, *How to Read a Poem and Fall in Love with Poetry* (Mariner, 1999).
_____, *The Essential Poet's Glossary* (Mariner, 2017).
David Holbrook, Christopher Middleton and David Wevil, *Penguin Modern Poets 4* (Penguin, 1965).
Ted Hughes, *Hawk in the Rain* (Faber Paperbacks, 1976).
_____, *Season Songs* (Faber & Faber, 1977).

James Joyce, *Pomes Penyeach* (Faber & Faber, 1968).
Juliana of Norwich, *Revelations of Divine Love* (Oxford University Press, 2015).
Jon Kabat-Zinn, *Wherever You Go, There You Are* (Hachette, 1994).
Jean Kein, *I Am* (New Sarum Press, 2021).
Frank Kermode (ed.), *The Selected Poetry of Marvell* (New American Library, 1967).
Philip Larkin, *Collected Poems* (Faber & Faber, 2003).
Ursula K. Le Guin, *The Wave in the Mind: Talks and Essays on the Writer, the Reader, and the Imagination* (Shambhala Publications Inc., 2004).
Audre Lorde, *Sister Outsider* (Penguin, 2019).
Hugh MacDiarmid, *Selected Poetry* (Fyfield Books, 2004).
Rachel Mann, *A Kingdom of Love* (Carcanet Press, 2019).
_____, *The Risen Dust* (Wild Goose Publications, 2013).
Susan Margrave, *Exculpatory Lilies* (McClelland & Stewart, 2022).
Ralph Maud & Aneirin Talfan Davies, *The Colour of Saying: An Anthology of Verse Spoken by Dylan Thomas* (Aldine Paperbacks, 1965).
Alastair McIntosh, *Riders on the Storm: The Climate Crisis and the Survival of Being* (Birlinn, 2021).
Alastair McIntyre, *After Virtue* (Duckworth Press, 1981).
Dorothy McMillan, Michael Byrne (eds.), *Modern Scottish Women Poets* (Canongate, 2003).
Jürgen Moltmann, *Theology and Joy* (SCM Press, 1973).
George Monbiot, *Feral: Rewilding the Land, Sea and Human Life* (Penguin, 2013).
Toni Morrison, *The Bluest Eye* (Vintage, 2019).
Flannery O'Connor, *The Violent Bear It Away* (Faber & Faber, 1960).
John O'Donohue, *Divine Beauty: The Invisible Embrace* (Banta, 2004).
_____, *Anam Cara: A Book of Celtic Wisdom* (Harper, 1996).

Further Reading

Mary Oliver, *American Primitive* (Little, Brown & Co., 1983).
Anne Pia, *Transitory* (Luath Press, 2018).
Charles Péguy, *Saints and Sinners: Prose and Poetry* (Cluny Media, 2019).
Marge Piercy, *The Crooked Inheritance* (Alfred A. Knopf, 2006).
Alison Phipps, *Call and No Response* (Wild Goose Publications, 2024).
Sylvia Plath, *Ariel* (Faber & Faber, 1965).
Joanna Ramsey, *The Seed Beneath the Snow: Remembering George MacKay Brown* (Sandstone Press, 2015).
Robin Robertson, *The Shadow's Gift* (Nicolas Hays, 2011).
Charlotte Rostek, *Scottish Women Artists* (Fleming Collection, 2024).
Carl Sagan and Ann Druyan, *Pale Blue Dot* (Ballantine, 1997).
Keith Sagar (ed.), *D. H. Lawrence Selected Poems* (Penguin, 1976).
Seigfried Sassoon, *Selected Poems* (Faber & Faber, 1968).
Barbara Schwepcke & Bill Swainson, *A New Divan: A Lyrical Dialogue between East and West* (Gingko, 2019).
Jill Segger, *Words Out of Silence* (Siglum, 2019).
Anna Deavere Smith, *Talk to Me: Listening Between the Lines* (Random House, 2001).
Oliver Soden, *Jeoffrey: The Poet's Cat* (The History Press, 2020).
_____, *Michael Tippett: The Biography* (Weidenfeld & Nicolson, 2019).
Mirabai Starr, *Ordinary Mysticism* (Collins, 2024).
Brian Stone, *Medieval English Verse* (Penguin, 1973).
John V. Taylor, *Enough is Enough* (SCM Press, 1972).
Michael Tippett, *Those Twentieth Century Blues: An Autobiography* (Hutchinson, 1991).
_____, *Music of the Angels: Essays and Sketches* (Eulenburg, 1980).
_____, *Moving into Aquarius* (Routledge & Kegan Paul, 1959).

Dylan Thomas, *In My Craft or Sullen Art* (Ragged Hand, 2024).
_____, *Miscellany Two* (J. M. Dent, 1974).
Nadia Tuéni, *Lebanon: Poems of Love and War* (Syracuse University Press, May 2006).
Suzanne Vega, *The Passionate Eye* (Harper, 2001).
Salley Vickers, *Miss Garnet's Angel* (HarperCollins, 2007).
Simone Weil, *Gravity and Grace* (Routledge Classics, 2002).
Rowan Williams, *The Edge of Words* (Bloomsbury Continuum, 2014).

Online Resources

Scottish Poetry Library – www.scottishpoetrylibrary.org.uk
National Poetry Library – www.southbankcentre.co.uk/venues/national-poetry-library/
Poetic Outlaws – https://poeticoutlaws.substack.com
Poem-a-Day – https://poets.org/poem-a-day
The Marginalian (Maria Popova) – https://www.themarginalian.org
The Poetry Foundation – www.poetryfoundation.org

More Creativity

Alison Croggon – https://alisoncroggon.com
Andy Kissane – http://andykissane.com
Kevin Scully – www.kevin-scully.com/poetry
Adey Grummet – https://www.adeygrummet.co.uk
Elspeth Murray – https://elspethmurray.com
Richard Medrington – https://www.richardmedrington.com
Diana Macalintal (liturgy.life) – https://liturgy.life
John O' Donohue – http://www.johnodonohue.com
Michael Tippett Musical Foundation – www.tippettfoundation.org.uk
Edinburgh Music Review – https://www.edinburghmusicreview.com
Pen Reid – https://penreid.co.uk/about
David Bentley Hart – https://davidbentleyhart.substack.com/

Further Reading

Tina Beattie – https://www.tinabeattie.com
Barbara Higbie – https://barbarahigbie.com
Judith I. Bridgland – http://www.jibridgland.com
Anne Butler – https://annebutlerart.com
James Donald – https://www.pickone.co.uk
Maria Vigers – https://www.mariavigers.com

Acknowledgements

If you're lucky enough to be an artist's muse, they will immortalise you. – Soledad Francis

THE TITLE of this collection, and of part three in particular, comes from a selection of liturgical material put out in 1981 (if I recall correctly) by the World Student Christian Federation. It was Vaughan Jones who first drew it to my attention. This is not the only way in which he has been important in my life. Thank you, Vaughan. Somehow, I have always felt that one day I would write a book called 'Living Beyond Our Means', exploring the significance of this too-often-inverted idea for orienting better in an over-commodified world. Here I have nearly succeeded. 'Living' may not be on the front cover, just 'beyond'. But hopefully the essence of what I am reaching out for runs through these pages.[1]

There are so many people to thank for helping make this collection possible. But one, in particular, stands out. I wish to express special gratitude to Lesley Wall for the evocative cover image, for providing inspiration for this project, for some valued (by me, anyway) conversations in 2023 and 2024, and for supporting my rediscovered poetic voice through moments of mutual kindness which I only wish could be more and many. The book as a whole is a gift to her (and to Ziggy), especially the opening and closing 'moon poems' (part of a larger, emerging set) and a number of others, principally in part two. Here lies the wound and the gift. As Maya Angelou once put it, "I wanted to be a rainbow in your

---

1 My earlier poetic efforts also had a liturgical connection: prayers and reflections in Geoffrey Duncan, *A World of Blessing* (Canterbury Press, 2000) and a number of other places.

cloud. Instead I added to the storm, and you headed for the shelter." For the time being.

Thanks also to several places and events where I was able to test run a few of these poems – not least the Hub (Edinburgh International Festival in 2023) and St James' Leith, for Advent and a Burns Supper. Ah, Rabbie… another voice from Scotland, which has invaded my soul. As someone once said, in Scotland poetry exists in the landscape, in ritual sites, in paths, greens, waters and landforms. These all carry stories, hiding in plain sight. There might have been more direct Scottish connections here. Next time.

One afternoon, out of curiosity, I sat down to write a list of all the poets I know personally, or who I have had communication with through email, the internet and social media. I was quite surprised by the number. Poetry seeps into all kinds of people and places. Long may it be so. I fear that I will have missed some good folk (apologies in advance), but those people for whom I am grateful as persons and in verse include, in democratically alphabetical order: Anne Booth, Beth Cross (for whose mutual encouragement I am extremely thankful), Graham Campbell, Jim Cotter (of blessed memory), Alison Croggon, Gilo, Adey Grummet, Bea Gonzalez, John Henson, Graham Kings, Andy Kissane, Rachel Mann, Alwyn Marriage, Danielle Macleod, Maria C. McCarthy, Richard Medrington, Adrian Mitchell, Janet Morley, Elspeth Murray, John O'Donohue (rest in the Light), Pádraig Ó Tuama, Alison Phipps, Maria Popova (an unending online treasury), Stephen Plaice, Pen Reid, Jill Segger, Kevin Scully, Richard Skinner, Hannah Ward, Stephen Watt, Alison Webster and Veronica Zundel. What a caravan of talent and inspiration.

Poetry and writing more generally also emerges from a whole web of friendship, life experience and life-sharing. Among the friends, allies, interlocutors and people who have touched me, who I remain grateful to, and who I wish to mention here, are: Priscilla Abbott (it's been a long time), Graham Adams, Nick Adams, Indra Adnan, Jo Aspinall, David and Sue Atkinson,

Acknowledgements

Carleen Anderson, Jonathan Bartley, Pat Bennett, Anna Bland, Wendy Bradley, Andrew and Helen Bradstock, Deidre Brock, Fiona Brocklesby, Domo Branch, Judith Bridgeland and lovely family, Sue Burkholder, Steve and Anne Butler, Bob Carling, Jane Carlton, Shaeron Caton-Rose, Julian Cheyne, Lisa Clark, Keith Clements, Alison Cobb, the Cooray-Smiths (Jim, Swyrie and Danuka), Jonathan Crawford, Katie Crumlish, Henrietta Cullinan, the Cunliffes, Norma Dalgleish and Fran Whitton, Paul Davies, Wilma Dickson, Ian Dommett, James Donald, Hazel Dunlop, Bonnie Evans-Hills, Lynn Failing, Janet Fife, Mark Fisher, Paul Fisher ('The Fire and the Rose'), Kai Funkschmidt, Andrew and Christine Galloway, John Gillibrand, Caroline Gilmour, Carrie Gooch (and in memory of Catherine), Deidre Good and Julian Sheffield, Paul Goodwin, Liz Goold, David Gow, Kate Guthrie, Harry Hagopian, Siân Harris, Gerry Hassan and Rosie Ilett, Innes Hatcher, Rhona Dyer Hatcher, Savi Hensman, Barbara Highbie, Symon Hill, David and Lorna Hoy, Chris Hudson, Tom Hurcombe, Doug Hynd, Fiona Jamieson, Vaughan Jones, Pat Kane, Hugh Kerr and Christine Twine (and all at *Edinburgh Music Review*), Karen King, Eleanor Kreider, Iain Lothian, Sandra MacRae, Sigrid Marten, Johan Maurer, Alastair McIntosh, Joyce McMillan, Bernadette Meaden, Mary Metzler and Gordon Prieb, Mary Miller, Roger Mitchell (*Kenarchy*), Robbie Mochrie, Virginia Moffatt and Chris Cole, Henry Morgan, Rachel Muers, Kevin Mulryne, Cathy Nelson, Will and Yvonne Newcombe, Lesley Orr, Sue Parfitt (and in memory of Graeme), Martyn Percy, Henry Potts, Ian and Rosalind Pusey, Milja Radovic, Ian Randall, Anne Richards, Clare Roberts and Aurélien Calmès, Margaret Roberts, Michael Roberts, Katrina Robinson, Chris Rowland, Peter Selby, Beth Seymour, Catherine Shea, Oliver Soden, Joey Sprague and Gary Brunk, Jared Stacy, Frank and Elea Strang, Steven Sullivan, the very special Tchilingirians (Jordan, Shona and Oshin), Priscilla Trenchard, Vic Theissen, Neill Walker, Shirley Wilson (in memory of Ian), Iain Whyte (in gratitude of Isobel), David Wostenholme (in memory of Andrew).

Since a number of the poems concern loss, I also wish to hold in gratitude here, and hold in the Light, some of the many who have passed through my life, who I miss dearly, and who shine on in eternal memory. Aside from those mentioned above, they include my beloved parents and grandparents (Leslie, Belle, Stanley and Florence), Betty and Chris Birch, Hilda Buckley, J. R. Burkholder, Ian and Margaret Fraser, Alasdair Galloway, Angela Gibson, Peter Hall, Catherine Harkin, Jenny Hill, Alan Kreider, Kenneth Leech, Fergus MacPherson, Jean Mayland, Ed and Ethel Metzler (and others within the US family), Colin M. Morris, Jocelyn Murray, Nigel Rogers, Ann Stricklen, Willard Swartley, Alan Wilson, Diana Witts, Jean Woods, and a host of other witnesses to goodness, truth and beauty in diverse ways. "They wound and they bless me with strange gifts: the salt of absence, the honey of memory" (Norman MacCaig).

Then, last but never least, there is my wife, Carla J. Roth, and her wonderful family to thank for their love and support. That includes Alice and Willard Roth, Kevin Roy Roth and Cindy Ritchie Roth (the regular Sunday Zoom crew) and their direct and indirect progeny.

May the verse be with you all.

About the Author

Simon Barrow is a writer, commentator, adult educator, activist, publisher and poet. He was until recently director of the beliefs, ethics and politics think-tank Ekklesia, and has formerly worked in a variety of creative roles in journalism, the ecumenical movement, politics and community-based education. He has written, edited and co-edited 17 books so far, ranging from Scottish and global current affairs to music and theology. In 2020 he co-edited and partly co-authored *Scotland After the Virus* (Luath Press), which prefaced its social commentary with newly commissioned poetry and short stories. The germ of an idea for this collection came from that book. Simon writes regularly for the Edinburgh Music Review, and he has published in a wide range of newspapers, magazines, journals and other periodicals over the past forty years. He moved to Scotland 15 years ago, and lives in Leith. His newsletter can be found at: https://substack.com/@simonbarrow. Simon's book *Transfiguring the Everyday: The Musical Vision of Michael Tippett* is also due to be published by Siglum.

Winter Sun

Leavened for a crisp Christmas morning
Each beam is a wheatfield of flames
Sending soft radiance earthwards
Letting the family gather anew
Extending their arms around
You, in the greeting glow of
Winter's windfall light…